THE
OTHER PREACHER
IN LYNCHBURG

For Janie,
fellow struggler
against injustice
and falsehoods,

John Killinger

ALSO BY JOHN KILLINGER

The Changing Shape of Our Salvation

Seven Things They Don't Teach You in Seminary

God, the Devil, and Harry Potter

Winter Soulstice: Celebrating the Spirituality of the Wisdom Years

Ten Things I Learned Wrong from a Conservative Church

God's People at Prayer

The Storybook Weddings of Mackinac Island

THE
OTHER PREACHER
IN LYNCHBURG

My Life Across Town from

Jerry Falwell

JOHN KILLINGER

THOMAS DUNNE BOOKS

ST. MARTIN'S PRESS ⚹ NEW YORK

THOMAS DUNNE BOOKS.
An imprint of St. Martin's Press.

THE OTHER PREACHER IN LYNCHBURG. Copyright © 2009 by John Killinger.
All rights reserved. Printed in the United States of America.
For information, address St. Martin's Press, 175 Fifth Avenue,
New York, N.Y. 10010.

www.thomasdunnebooks.com
www.stmartins.com

Library of Congress Cataloging-in-Publication Data

Killinger, John.
    The other preacher in Lynchburg: my life across town from Jerry Falwell/John
Killinger.—1st ed.
        p. cm.
    ISBN-13: 978-0-312-53858-3
    ISBN-10: 0-312-53858-8
    1. Killinger, John. 2. Baptists—United States—Clergy—Biography.
I. Title.
BX6495.K483A3   2009
285'.1092—dc22
    [B]   2008036236

First Edition: March 2009

10   9   8   7   6   5   4   3   2   1

FOR JACK T. COSBY,

a citizen without guile,

a friend without flaw,

and a man whom I loved

above most other men

CONTENTS

Six

Seven

Epilogue

ACKNOWLEDGMENTS

When the definitive story of Rev. Jerry Falwell is finally written, the author or authors will turn to two important figures, Professor James J. H. Price and Professor William Goodman, longtime members of the religion department at Lynchburg College. Presbyterian ministers who belonged to what were then called Blue Ridge and Shenandoah Presbyteries and attended the church I pastored from 1980 to 1986, Jim and Bill had begun their tracking of Falwell long before I arrived on the scene and had published a book called *Jerry Falwell: An Unauthorized Profile,* whose distinctive feature was that it exhibited, side by side, numerous examples of the famous evangelist's public utterances in which he contradicted himself when speaking to different audiences. They were able to assemble this volume because they had carefully audited Falwell's weekly radio and TV sermons as well as his frequent off-the-cuff statements to local, state, and national reporters. These extremely perceptive culture watchers had an uncanny prescience about Falwell's significance to American religion and dedicated themselves to the preservation of materials that will eventually afford the truest assessment of his character and significance as founder and principal figure of Thomas Road Baptist Church, the *Old-Time Gospel Hour,* Liberty Baptist College (later Liberty University), and the Moral Majority, as well as the erstwhile hijacker of the *PTL Club* and Heritage USA, Jim and Tammy Faye Bakker's charismatic empire.

Because he served part-time on the staff of our church, Jim Price in particular often shared with me the latest news of what was happening in the Falwell camp and provided me with tapes of Falwell's sermons and extemporaneous remarks just as they were delivered in his church and not as later edited for television. He and Bill were also extremely supportive of my own efforts to understand and critique Falwell's place in American religious life during one of the crucial final decades of the twentieth century. Without what I learned from them, I would never have undertaken the writing of this book. I am grateful for their tutelage, their optimism, and their ever-cheerful demeanor—their very *Christian* spirit!—during an unusually challenging period of my life.

I would be remiss if I didn't also say a good word for the

entire membership of the First Presbyterian Church of Lynchburg, a distinguished old congregation to whom I was naturally drawn by their unfailing kindness, old-world civility, and all-around goodwill. No minister could ever receive a more generous and unstinting acceptance of his preaching and leadership than I did. Only one parishioner, a fine, well-meaning lady named Johnnie Lu Morgan, ever chided me for preaching sermons aimed at the Moral Majority, the *Old-Time Gospel Hour,* and television evangelism in general, and she did so because she believed—correctly!—that every sermon is a singular opportunity for proclaiming the gospel, not for talking about what is wrong with those who are failing to do it.

My wife, Anne, and I were blessed during our six-year pastorate in Lynchburg to have hosts of dear friends, whose names, if I listed all of them, would require a great deal of space. Therefore I shall name only a few.

There were Jack and Anne Cosby, who were so instrumental in our moving to Lynchburg and continued to befriend us as long as we were there; Eloise Snead and Dora Evans, both invaluable secretaries at the church; Robert and Jo Anne Snell, whose lives became ensnared in ministry, so that Bob eventually became an associate minister at Brick Presbyterian Church in New York and is now senior minister of a large, active church in Lincoln, Nebraska; Audie Goldenberg, Margaret Crist, and Deanne Gwaltney, all older, mothering figures whose cheerful mien invariably lifted our hearts; Bob and Jean Fortune and their daughter, Suzanne, who always welcomed us with open arms to their gracious country home; George Stewart, the funny, worldly-wise president and CEO of First Colony Life Insurance, and his quiet, lovely wife, Bonnie; Dan and Deborah Raessler, both teachers at Randolph Macon Woman's College, who shared their fabulous children, Jonathan and Sarah Margaret, with us; Dr. David Hill and his wife, Judy, who had been a dear friend of Anne's even before our time in Lynchburg; Warren and Priscilla Light, who left us for a couple of years to become missionary workers in Taiwan and have in recent years become two of our dearest friends.

Nor can I fail to mention the jolly, upbeat members of our "birthday club," which met monthly to celebrate one another's birthdays or, when there was no birthday, simply to have a good time. These close and loving friends included Ken and Gail Kowalski, Bob and Nancy Glenn, Jim and Marian Price, Betty Jo Kendall (who is now Betty Jo Hamner), Dick and Genny Harris, and Ed and Jean Moyer. Ken, who was a former school superintendent and understood the pressure often produced by public stands, was a particularly helpful counselor. Dick and Ed are now deceased, and Jean, who in her eighties is as pretty as ever, was the extraordinarily competent and devoted secretary who allowed me to do three times the work I might otherwise have accomplished.

It is hard to believe, remembering that period after a lapse of almost a quarter of a century, how many wonderful friends and acquaintances we had in Lynchburg, and how their images still have the power to flood our hearts and souls with joy.

One dear lady unknown to us during those Lynchburg years because she was hard at work as an editor in New York City is our special friend Ruth Cavin, who has lent her gentle wisdom and angel touch to improving this book. Long known as the Queen of Mystery Editors because of her ability to encourage prize-winning whodunits, Ruth possesses an incredibly wide range of talents and interests, and has in recent years, in addition to editing my *God, the Devil, and Harry Potter,* developed books on themes as varied as bread making, Zen Buddhism, and the art of being a veterinarian. At ninety, she is a veritable treasure to St. Martin's Press, and, with the assistance of her highly valued lieutenant, Toni Plummer, appears fully prepared to continue working toward the century mark. I am grateful to both of them for seeing my manuscript through its various stages of editing and publishing, and hereby exonerate them from any faults in the finished product while happily acknowledging their numerous improvements on it.

Thanks, each and every one of you. As St. Paul was wont to say when writing to his friends in the many places where he established churches, "I thank my God on every remembrance of you!"

I never get mad in a fight. I don't care who they are, give me a few weeks or months with them, and they'll be my friend.

—Jerry Falwell, cited by Deborah Caldwell in "Jerry Falwell and Me"

My mother always told me that no matter how much you dislike a person, when you meet them face-to-face you will find characteristics about them that you like. Jerry Falwell was a perfect example of that. I hated everything he stood for, but after meeting him in person years after the trial, Jerry Falwell and I became good friends. He would visit me in California and we would debate together on college campuses. I always appreciated his sincerity even though I knew what he was selling and he knew what I was selling.

—Larry Flynt, owner of *Hustler* magazine, whom Falwell sued for defamation of character

THE
OTHER PREACHER
IN LYNCHBURG

Introduction

The day Jerry Falwell died, May 15, 2007, I began being deluged by phone calls and e-mails from friends and acquaintances all over the United States, mostly ministers, reminding me of this or that story I had told them about my years as a pastor in Lynchburg, Virginia, Falwell's town.

"You should write a book about him," many said.

My wife, Anne, and I were sad to hear that he had died. At least Anne was sad. She kept remarking that she thought it strange I was not more sad. Finally I had to explain it to her, and perhaps to myself.

I said, "I am sad, but not in the usual way. I think it's for an era as much as a man—for all the things he did in his life-time, for the way he was always opening his mouth and put-ting his foot in it. For what he did to shape the political life of America as we know it. It's as if a great ship has gone down, or an icon has passed."

I kept thinking of Vachel Lindsay's poem "General William Booth Enters into Heaven," and wondered if Fal-well's entering heaven was anything like that. I know there were some people who thought he wouldn't go to heaven when he died, but I'm more charitable. Somewhere inside the big, boisterous preacher and disputationist was a little boy who enjoyed Christmas trees and practical jokes and crab-leg sandwiches—he introduced me to crab-leg sandwiches—and I could only imagine him blinking his eyes at all the sights he was likely to be seeing in heaven, like a starry-eyed waif who had a lot to learn but was wide open to doing it. There was no way he was in hell, even if I believed in a traditional hell, which I don't.

My time in Lynchburg was only six years. Six years in the 1980s, when Falwell was at the top of his form. He had just started the Moral Majority, he had helped to elect President Reagan, his college was in its early days, his buses were haul-ing in people from large areas of Virginia, his office was a bee-hive of activity, he was in the news almost daily, he was tasting power and finding it heady, and he was as full of sass and en-ergy as a new pup. In 1983, *Good Housekeeping* magazine's national poll rated him the second most respected man in America, just behind President Reagan. If I could have cho-sen any six years of my life to be there, those were the ones.

On a scale of one to ten, my influence on Falwell, one way or another, was probably only a point-five or less. His influence on me was—well, that's part of the story I want to tell. I never became one of his followers. That's clear to anyone who knows me. But running into him at that stage of his career, and at precisely that point in my own, when I had just left fifteen years of teaching in a divinity school to become the pastor of a large church in the city he controlled, certainly made a difference in my trajectory. It didn't turn me around, but it did knock me a few degrees off course.

As I say in the book, I think it's what really made a theologian out of me, by forcing me to think about what Falwell was saying and doing and how it was affecting the shape of religion and life in America. There is no doubt in anybody's mind that he was a seminal force. Single-handedly, or at least more than anybody else, he was responsible for forging the religious right into a formidable political bloc in America. He helped to make Ronald Reagan president, and then to elect George H. W. Bush as his successor. He was the Great Polarizer, who bequeathed us the radically divided society we live with today.

I'm not really keen to relive those years in Lynchburg. I've always been a fairly passive, noncombative person to have gotten a reputation across the years for being an upstart and a rebel. It offended something deep in my nature to have to stand up to Falwell and his kind of theology. But I was there—I sometimes thought maybe God had planned it that way—and somebody had to do it.

At first, I resisted the idea of taking a stroll down that

particular section of memory lane. I preferred to forget it, and let bygones be bygones. The country has moved on, theology has moved on, I have moved on.

But the more I thought about it, the more I realized I probably knew one aspect of Jerry Falwell as well as anybody alive. I was sitting on the fifty-yard line when he was at the top of his game, and it would be remiss of me not to share what I saw and felt at that time. As a fellow clergyman in Lynchburg, I knew things about Falwell most Americans didn't know and couldn't understand if they did. Maybe I had an obligation to talk about those things.

So I decided to write this book as my memoir about a man I would have been glad to have as a friend if he hadn't been so wary of anybody who had a better education than he did or spoke from a more sophisticated theological position. I liked Jerry Falwell. He had a puckish, bad-boy way about him that made him likable. He was extremely charismatic, and radiated an energy that naturally attracted people. But we got off on the wrong foot—more about that later—and he never really trusted me enough to be friends. So we remained opponents, he in his corner and I in mine.

What I have written, however, is out of respect, not disrespect. Respect for Falwell's enormous energy. Respect for his unbelievable chutzpah. Respect for the incredible verve that enabled him to build and lead a coalition of conservative forces for enough years to alter America's history and destiny. Respect for his legacy—a large church and even larger university that are now the economic mainstay of the town that was always his home.

I also feel respect for a core of real faith and belief the man had, and for the blind doggedness that allowed him to go on being who he was, and being happy with that, even after his poll numbers had plummeted and he was ridiculed by sizable numbers of people, especially gays and lesbians and liberal journalists.

I won't cut the cloth to flatter his figure. On the contrary, I will call things just the way I saw them then and still see them today. But I shall say what I have to say over against the iconic stature of a man who, unlike so many celebrities and public figures, was really who he appeared to be, and, once his course was set, rarely altered it to suit his critics.

ONE

Choosing Lynchburg

I had grown up in the Southern Baptist tradition and always intended to be a pastor, not a teacher. Things being what they were in the South, though, my training at Harvard Divinity School was suspect—as was my having earned a Ph.D. in English literature before going to Harvard—and I wasn't called to a church. So I had come back South as a professor of English in Georgetown College, a small Baptist school in Kentucky. After two years at Georgetown, I had gone to Princeton Theological Seminary to work with Paul Scherer, a famous Lutheran homiletician, and ended up with another kind of doctorate. I didn't realize it, but I was only putting myself farther and farther from "callability" by a Baptist congregation.

From Princeton I went to Louisville to be the academic dean of a new liberal arts college—one with Baptist origins—but my heart wasn't really in academics, it was still in being a pastor. So when I had an opportunity to go to Vanderbilt University as a professor in the divinity school, I lost no time in accepting it. At least I would be working with preachers, and, who knew, I might one day end up as pastor of a church.

Vanderbilt and Nashville, where it is located, were a wonderful interlude in my life and the lives of my family, which now included, in addition to my wife, Anne, two sons, Eric and Krister. We built a lovely new house in Nashville, the boys attended fantastic private schools, I was invited to speak in more venues than I could possibly accept, we spent two academic years and several summers abroad, I wrote a number of books, and I had many bright and capable students, some of whom I still enjoy as friends.

One of the most important aspects of life at Vanderbilt was its strong sense of ecumenism, which enabled me to grow from being a Baptist into being a Christian-in-general, without respect to denomination. That was just as well, as I had a run-in with the Southern Baptist Sunday School Board in Nashville only a year after going to Vanderbilt.

I was speaking to a large student conference at Golden Gate Baptist Theological Seminary in Mill Valley, California, one of five Southern Baptist seminaries. My first address—the program committee had assigned the title for it—was called "Christ in a World of Revolution." In my second address, "Christ *Is* a Revolution"—my own title—I made a few seconds' worth of remarks about the denominational slavishness exhibited by the Sunday School Board, where several of my friends worked. My friends' thoughts and writings, I knew, were constantly reviewed and bowdlerized before reaching the public. The response, from the school's president as well as from Sunday School Board officials, was as outraged and instantaneous as if I had whipped out a machine gun and mown down everybody on the speaker's platform.

It was my first real experience with bureaucracy and how quickly it moves to cover and protect itself. First, the Southern Baptist Sunday School Board sent out a web of fabricated reports and news releases accusing me of everything from inaccuracy to immorality. (I had used an illustration from a James Baldwin novel; ipso facto, I was almost certainly a homosexual.) It canceled my future speaking engagements in the denomination and threatened to withhold funding from institutions that hosted me. Later, it even circulated false stories to the effect that I had begged the pardon of the Sunday School Board's executive secretary, wept before a large audience over the error of my ways, and had been graciously embraced and forgiven.

Employees of the board, moreover, were secretly warned that they would be dismissed if seen associating with me. As a result, several close friends in the church we belonged to no longer spoke to us, and others took every precaution against detection when communicating with us. Our lives as Baptists were suddenly, peremptorily, and definitively over.

From then on, we would be ecumenists whether we wished to be or not.

Despite the overall happiness of our lives in Nashville, though, I began at midlife to desire what many men desire in that period of their lives—to revisit earlier vocational pathways and possibly resume one of those. I had become a highly successful young academic. I was widely known, had won grants to study abroad, had been promoted to full professor, and had published several books. But I found myself yearning again to be a pastor, and to fulfill my earlier sense of calling as a minister. I had at various times entertained invitations to become the minister of several large, progressive churches—in North Carolina, New York, and Minnesota—and had dismissed them without a thought. Now, in my middle years, I became very serious about making a change.

I talked with congregations in Houston, Grand Rapids, Denver, Los Angeles, and then, almost reluctantly, Lynchburg, Virginia. I was very much attracted to the church in Los Angeles, and was on the verge of accepting its invitation, when a winsome, late-middle-aged man named Jack Cosby and his wife, Anne, showed up at a statewide Disciples of Christ conference where I was speaking in Gatlinburg, Tennessee. They were from the First Presbyterian Church of Lynchburg, Virginia, Jack confided in his soft voice, and would be grateful if I would meet them for breakfast.

"No," said Anne. "You're not interested in going to Lynchburg. Let's not take our breakfast hour in this lovely place to meet with them."

"You're only afraid I'll listen to them," I said.

"You will," she said. "I know you will."

She was right.

Jack Cosby was one of the most inviting, irresistible men I ever met. Tall, slightly bent, and rough-hewn—I often thought of him as "Lincolnesque"—he wasn't physically attractive. In fact, he was almost the opposite. But he had such a kind heart and such a gentle civility about him that I couldn't say no to his invitation to visit Lynchburg and talk with their search committee. Before we left Gatlinburg, we had arranged a date for the visit.

Anne and I drove to Lynchburg with a sense of its being a doomed visit from the start. I knew almost nothing about Lynchburg except, as I could tell from the map, it seemed to sit in the middle of nowhere. There was no major institution of learning there, the nearest real theater and music were three hours away, in Washington, D.C., and the town's only claim to fame, as far as I could tell, was that it was the home of Jerry Falwell, who was somehow connected to the newly formed Moral Majority, about which I knew very little and cared less.

"We'll go for a couple of days," I told Anne. "Then we'll drive home. It will give us a chance to get away and do some thinking. We can consider moving to that church in L.A."— which is what I fully expected us to do.

The search committee members at First Presbyterian were all lovely, cultivated people who knew exactly how to appeal to my sympathies. They had been looking for a new pastor for two years. At the end of the first year, they had identified someone they wanted, but, after agreeing to come, he changed his mind and remained with his church in Florida.

They told a lot of funny stories about their experiences going into other churches to listen to prospective preachers.

In one town, they arrived early, parked a couple of blocks from the church, and made their ways individually to the church and sat in different parts of the sanctuary so they would not be recognized as a search committee. But the pastor they were there to scrutinize, unaware of their mission and wishing to be hospitable, asked all visitors to stand and tell the congregation where they were from. Sheepishly, one by one, they confessed that they were from Lynchburg, Virginia.

The congregants soon realized there was a predatory committee in their midst and broke out in laughter. It was an awkward moment, but the people were so nice to the visitors that it overcame their embarrassment.

And when they had heard him preach, they decided they didn't want that minister after all!

Another time, when they had flown to Florida to eavesdrop on another minister, two young men on the committee went out to a roadhouse for a beer. As they stood at the bar, an attractive young woman came up to the handsomer of the two, a businessman named Jim Christian, and asked him to dance. They were on the dance floor when she asked Jim where he was from. He told her.

"Oh," she said, "you're a long way from home. What are you doing down here?"

"You wouldn't believe it if I told you," he said, lazily gyrating to the music.

"Try me," she said.

"I'm with a church pulpit nominating committee," he said. "We're here to look at a minister."

Suddenly, the woman stopped dancing and stood absolutely still, studying Jim's face. Deciding that he was telling the truth, she promptly turned on her heels and walked away, deserting him in the middle of the floor.

I liked those people. Every one of them. I liked it that they had a sixteen-year-old boy, Ed Richards, on the committee, and that they let him talk and listened to him as if what he said was as important as anything the rest of them said. A couple of elderly women were on the committee too, and they were accorded the same courtesy.

There were also a financial adviser, the owner of a large roofing company, a leather broker, a doctor's wife, a nuclear scientist's wife, a teacher, an attorney's wife, a department store executive, and of course Jack Cosby, who was president of the American Federal Savings and Loan Association.

Jack also happened to be the brother of Gordon Cosby, the minister who founded the famous Church of the Savior in Washington, D.C.—celebrated in Elizabeth O'Connor's book *Call to Commitment*—and whose wife, Mary Cosby, was a well-known inspirational speaker. Mary and I had been together on a program for a large gathering of United Methodist pastors in Macon, Georgia, and it was she who had given my name to Jack.

There were four Cosby brothers, all of whom except Jack became ministers, and one sister, Mary Gordon Cosby, who married a minister. One of the brothers, Beverly, had founded an ecumenical fellowship in Lynchburg called the Church of the Covenant that operated along the same lines as Gordon's church in Washington, requiring members to pray and study the Scriptures daily, tithe their incomes, and become regularly engaged in ministries for the poor and homeless. I remember saying once from my pulpit at First Presbyterian Church that, pound for pound, it was the finest church in Lynchburg.

I think Jerry Falwell was mentioned only one time in all the hours I spent with the search committee. I asked if his being in Lynchburg affected life at First Presbyterian Church. Falwell was on the other side of town, they said, and they hardly ever thought about him. They were too busy living their own lives, tending to their own problems, trying to be a church in their own way. They didn't speak ill of Falwell or his ministry. It was just that he didn't seem relevant to their existence.

They were smart. When we got home, the phone rang. One of the men on the committee wanted to speak to our boys, who were then sixteen and nineteen. He said, "We're talking to your dad and mom about moving to Lynchburg. We think you ought to see Lynchburg for yourselves so you'll know what that might mean to you."

They invited our sons to fly to Lynchburg, at their expense, and spend a long weekend with them. The boys were delighted, and felt very important. When they got there, the committee wined and dined them just as they had us. They took them down to Smith Mountain Lake for a night or two. Jack and Anne Cosby had a lovely home there, and an amphibious car, one that ran on land and on the water as well. The boys had a great time "driving" across the lake.

They came home and said, "Dad, you've got to go to Lynchburg!"

When I prayed about what I should do, that was the message I got too: I had to go to Lynchburg.

I was flabbergasted, because I had had no intention of going there. But I knew it was what I had to do.

For those who have never been in the Christian ministry or had close relatives who are, I should explain something. Ministers often do things that seem irrational or unexplainable. It has to do with their faith, and the sense that they are fulfilling their destiny by going where they are sent regardless of their personal desires or logic of purpose.

All the little arrows in my head were flashing toward Los Angeles. It was a larger church, it was in a major city, it offered a much more impressive stipend and a lot more opportunities for the family. But I knew, the way ministers do, that I was supposed to go to Lynchburg.

It was crazy. It was wild. It was illogical. But that was where I was supposed to go.

Lynchburg in 1980 was a sleepy little town of 67,000 nestled beside the James River on the eastern edge of the Blue Ridge Mountains. The largest town in the United States that wasn't on or near an interstate highway, it had lost its bid for a regional airport to Roanoke, some fifty miles away. Its own dinky little airport was serviced primarily by commuter planes flying north or south between Charlotte and Raleigh. A friend said when he heard we were moving to Lynchburg, "You'll love the restaurant at the airport. But be sure to take plenty of quarters." He was referring, of course, to the snack machines.

Like Rome, the city was built on seven hills. The roads and streets, viewed from the air at night when they were outlined by streetlights, traced crazy-quilt, unpredictable patterns that looked like the wild scribblings of a child on a tablet. That was because they followed the horse and cow paths around the many smaller hills instead of heading directly toward distant objectives. I never quite got the hang of them, and often found myself having to turn around and go in a different direction because I'd taken the wrong street.

Frances FitzGerald, in a *New Yorker* article in 1981, created an accurate portrait of Lynchburg. "The vista from the top of its one twenty-story building," she wrote, "is mainly of trees and a bend in the river." Despite the fact that there were about two hundred small factories in the town, she said, there wasn't much traffic, and on Sunday almost all the cars in town were parked near its churches.

It was a beautiful little city, with lots of antebellum houses and wonderful, ancient trees. Main Street, which was essentially the only business street downtown, ran through several blocks of old brick buildings, now mostly occupied by insurance agencies, antique stores, and small eateries, then west across a gorge, up the hill via Rivermont Avenue into what had once been an elegant section of big houses, out past Randolph-Macon College and Baptist Hospital, where it became Boonsboro Road, and continued for several miles past a small shopping center and Boonsboro Country Club into the foothills of the Blue Ridge. First Presbyterian Church sat on an expansive green campus just off the junction of Boonsboro Road and Virginia Episcopal School Road. Everything about this end of town was quiet, wooded, sedate, and laid-back.

Thomas Road Baptist Church and the rest of Falwell's empire lay on the other side of town, just off a short bypass road connecting the town's only real mall and most of the city's motels and restaurants. The people on our end of town went over there to shop, but the people on that end seldom came out to our neighborhood except when they needed to use the Baptist Hospital. Most of the doctors in town—Lynchburg had an unusually fine cadre of physicians—lived out our way, most of the laboring classes the other way.

The biggest thing that had ever happened to Lynchburg was the advent some twenty-five years earlier of General Electric, which quickly became the city's largest employer. The opening of the G.E. plant had necessitated the influx of hundreds of managers and manufacturing personnel from Northern cities such as Syracuse, New York, and most of the inhabitants of the city still referred to these folks as "the newcomers." Some even used the term "carpetbaggers." Until the arrival of the G.E. plant, the largest business in the area was the Craddock-Terry Shoe Corporation, one of the most respectable old manufacturing businesses in southwestern Virginia.

My secretary, Mrs. Jean Moyer, was from Syracuse. Her husband, Ed, was an engineer at Wiley & Wilson Engineering Firm. They didn't mind being called newcomers. In fact, they laughed about it. They liked the Southern ambience of Lynchburg—the milder winters, the gracious lifestyle, the quieter surroundings, the fact that you could really see the stars at night. Jean brought a Northern efficiency to her job. She was one of the best secretaries a minister ever had.

Jerry Falwell had grown up in Lynchburg. He was born in 1933, the year when I was born. His father was a notorious alcoholic, and, according to Jerry, an unbeliever almost to the end of his life. Jerry went to Lynchburg College, the four-year liberal arts college operated by the Christian Church (Disciples of Christ), but dropped out after two years. (He would later ask the president of the school for an honorary degree, but the president declined.) He then went to Baptist Bible College in Springfield, Missouri, a nonaccredited institution that promulgated a fundamentalist brand of religion and, like many such schools, insisted that true accreditation was in the eyes of the Lord, not at the whim of some earthly academic association.

Returning to Lynchburg, he started his own church with thirty-five members who had decided to separate from Park Avenue Baptist Church and called him as their pastor. By his own testimony, he spent many hours a day calling on homes in the area and inviting people to come to church. Within a year there were enough members to enable them to buy an old bottling warehouse and move into it, and eventually they erected their own church building. Then, ever the huckster, Falwell got the idea of buying a fleet of old school buses and using them to ferry crowds of people, mostly children and elderly people, to Sunday school and worship.

I have said that he was part used-car salesman. He had a deep, resonant voice that he loved to employ at full throttle and an expressive face that encouraged people to believe in whatever he believed in. He also knew the power of advertising, and how important it was to give people the idea that his church was the hottest thing since colored straws. Soon he was on the radio, and then television. The *Old-Time Gospel Hour,* his signature program, emanated from Thomas Road Baptist Church, and its format, reminiscent of Charles E. Fuller's *Old Fashioned Revival Hour,* with lots of music and special guest soloists, was soon the envy of evangelicals all over the country.

Lynchburgers were duly proud of their native son as he began to put their town on the map. Most of them never attended Thomas Road Baptist Church, but they knew who Jerry Falwell was and that he was going places. He had big ideas, and he was beginning to make waves on his side of town.

He had a natural gift for cultivating important people, locally as well as on the national scene.

One of the locals was Carter Glass III, publisher of the *Lynchburg News and Advance.* Falwell bought ads from Glass and convinced him that he was God's specially anointed servant. Bishop John Shelby Spong, a former Lynchburg pastor himself, in an article posted on his Web site after Falwell's death, recalled that Glass was a member of his parish, St. John's Episcopal, but thought Falwell was the only trustworthy preacher in town. Glass and Falwell agreed on many things. They believed that communism was a continuing danger to the United States, and that integration of the races was a communist plot to destroy the nation. Just as Randolph Hearst had told the reporters of his newspaper chain to "puff" Billy Graham at the beginning of his career, Glass was determined to exalt Jerry Falwell as a modern-day prophet who could save America if Americans would only listen to him.

Another local bigwig Falwell courted and won over was George Stewart, president of First Colony Life Insurance Company. George was a member of my church, First Presbyterian. He was a fascinating human being, a short, jolly, round-figured man who loved showing photographs of the skinny long-distance runner he had been in his college years. A successful New York businessman, he was summoned to Lynchburg to rescue an ailing insurance business, and in a short time turned it around and made it the largest life insurance company in the country.

An earnest Christian, George had acquired a library of religious books that was the envy of every preacher who saw it. His study, which occupied the entirety of a large, thickly carpeted basement beneath the spacious house he and his wife designed and built, was surrounded by shelves of expensive encyclopedia sets and biblical commentaries. In the evenings, he usually sat there at an oversize desk, studying his Bible and preparing the popular lessons he taught each Sunday morning to the men's Bible class at our church.

George was a humorous man, and despite his cheerful disposition was, I believe, deeply cynical about human beings. But he thought a lot of Falwell, served on the board of Liberty Baptist College, and made frequent public appearances on Liberty's campus. He seemed to like me as well and, oddly enough, never once upbraided me for things I said about the Moral Majority and TV evangelists. Yet I was never completely certain about what George was thinking, and often wondered if Falwell was also uncertain about where he stood with him. It may have been part of George's success, that he was able to be nice to people without fully revealing what was going on in his mind.

Eventually, George would become one of the richest men in Lynchburg, if not absolutely the richest. When First Colony Life Insurance Company was acquired by Ethyl Corporation, George told me that he had made more than $50 million personally in the transaction. He also became CEO of First Colony and a member of Ethyl's board, doubtless at some incredibly extravagant salary.

He was very generous with our church, and with the Blue Ridge Presbytery, of which our church was a member. But he was also exceedingly generous with Falwell, and made a number of large donations over the years to the *Old-Time Gospel Hour* and Liberty Baptist College.

George Stewart was important to Falwell in an additional way. In the early 1970s, Thomas Road Baptist Church and the *Old-Time Gospel Hour* had issued $6.5 million worth of bonds at very attractive interest rates. Falwell himself had hawked most of these bonds to viewers of the *OTGH* program. Then, as the bonds began coming due, Thomas Road

Baptist Church defaulted on them. It was their practice, according to common knowledge in Lynchburg, to send letters to the holders of the bonds, just as the bonds were coming due, saying they were very sorry, they were unable to pay the amount due, but could, if the holders were willing to settle for it, pay half of what was due. In other words, either the holders took half or got nothing.

In 1972, the United States Securities and Exchange Commission investigated the allegations of misdeed and charged Thomas Road Baptist Church with "fraud and deceit" in the issuance of the bonds. A year later, an appeals court ruled that there had been no institutional wrongdoing or criminal intention in the mishandling of funds. The judge, wishing to save thousands of creditors from financial harm, devised a creative way to rescue the embattled church. He appointed a five-man committee to oversee TRBC's finances until they were on sounder footing, and this committee reorganized the institution's debts, in part by issuing new bonds at attractive rates of interest. These highly desirable new bonds were snapped up by a lot of eager businessmen in Lynchburg.

George Stewart was chairman of this committee, and, I am sure, acquired thousands of dollars' worth of bonds for his own portfolio. Half the important businesspeople of Lynchburg bought into the scheme, not only saving Falwell and TRBC's bacon but ensuring that the business community itself would then do everything they could to protect the institution from future default.

I was reminded many times during my ensuing contest

with Falwell that I had no right to come into Lynchburg and threaten their money tree!

There were also dark rumors in Lynchburg at the time of our arrival concerning the death of one of Falwell's associates, a former member of his board of ministry named F. William "Bill" Menge. Two award-winning reporters, L. J. Davis and Ernest Volkman, published an article called "Jerry Falwell" in the November 1981 issue of *Penthouse* magazine that described Menge as a "confidence man and convicted tax evader, sometime associate of known drug smugglers," and a "former Falwell ministry board member and adviser."

(He was also a friend, they pointed out, of evangelists James Robison, Pat Robertson, and Kenneth Copeland.)

Menge was reputed to have been negotiating for the purchase of Ambassador College in Big Sandy, Texas, from the Worldwide Church of God for $10.6 million to build a Christian City there, complete with its own airport. He had made several trips to Israel, where he was in touch with Israeli mobsters and officials at El Al airlines about establishing a special airline to carry thousands of Christian tourists annually from Texas to the Holy Land. It was rumored, said the article, that he had first been attempting to establish this Christian City for Jerry Falwell, then for James Robison, and finally for Brother Lester Roloff, a Texas evangelist who gave him $500,000 that Roloff never saw again.

There was also gossip, said Davis and Volkman, that Menge's real interest in the Christian City with an airport

was to use it as a cover for flying in marijuana and other illegal substances from Mexico, and this was why he was involv-
ing the Israeli gangsters in the enterprise. It wasn't long after
this that law enforcement officials acknowledged that Tyler,
the closest large city to Big Sandy, Texas, had become a major
hub for the distribution of illegal drugs from Mexico.

As the reporters told the story, shortly after noon on Sep-
tember 6, 1980, Menge had taken his tractor to a piece of
property adjoining his own, an old farm in Forest, Virginia,
near Lynchburg, to bush-hog the grass so his children could
have a picnic on it. When his body was subsequently found
mangled beneath the Bush Hog, his left hand and right fore-
arm severed, his right leg nearly amputated, and his skull
fractured, it was surmised that he had encountered a buried
stump or utility pole that caused the tractor to lurch, throw-
ing him off beneath the churning tines of the Bush Hog.
But the tractor was still in high gear, suggesting that the
Bush Hog had not actually been working at the time, for it
would normally have been operating in low gear.

This terrible "accident" happened just days after Menge,
who had either resigned from or been forced off Falwell's
board of ministry, was quoted as saying he was going to "tell
all" and that people were "going to jail."

Two FBI agents, said Davis and Volkman, "briefly investigated" the bizarre case, but when the reporters attempted
to question authorities at the FBI they could get no information about the investigation or even a reason for the
FBI's being involved, as the incident would not normally
have fallen under its jurisdiction. And as the evidence of

foul play was only circumstantial, no one was ever charged with murder.

Still, the whole affair left a cloud of suspicion over Falwell, TRBC, *OTGH,* and their dealings. I personally heard rumors that two men from Falwell's organization had shown up at Menge's home shortly before the accident and had been told he was on his tractor in the neighboring field. Later, when Menge did not come home for dinner, his wife or another member of his family who went in search discovered his body lying beneath the Bush Hog on level ground.

According to the *Penthouse* reporters, Menge had swindled more than $9 million during the last few years from churches, banks, ministers, and individuals—which seemed odd in light of the fact that he was reputed to be nearly broke at the time of his death and there was no record of where the money had gone.

I did not personally believe Jerry Falwell was involved in criminal activities, but I was aware that there were often shady figures lurking in the background of big-time evangelism because of the enormous sums of money it generated. A former employee of Tulsa evangelist Oral Roberts, a man named Wayne Robinson, wrote a book about skullduggery in the Roberts organization, and suspicious characters were known to float in and out of the company of Jim and Tammy Bakker at the *PTL Club,* whose headquarters was in Charlotte, North Carolina.

One of my own divinity school students when I was at Vanderbilt, a large, imposing, darkly handsome, and theatrically inclined man named Larry Clifton, was invited during his final months of seminary to fly to New Jersey, all expenses paid, to meet with some people who wanted to bankroll him as a TV evangelist. Larry had earned money to pay his way through divinity school by being a professional wrestler and had apparently come to the men's attention for this reason. He and I talked about his meeting before he went, and I warned him that it seemed extremely suspicious for a group of businessmen to want to "create" an evangelist of their own. It certainly didn't sound like a legitimately Christian enterprise.

"You were right, Prof," said Larry in his flip way when he returned. "Those guys are Mafia. They're hoods! I could tell by the way they talked and acted. I'm a tough enough guy, but those fellows scared the living daylights out of me!"

So my take on Lynchburg was a very mixed one, even from our first weeks in town. It appeared to be a lovely haven for families. Most children who grew up there gradually drifted back from whatever universities and graduate schools they attended. The local public schools were good. There were two fine liberal arts institutions, Randolph-Macon College and Lynchburg College, and a third, nationally known Sweet Briar College, was only a dozen miles to the north, in the tiny town of Amherst. The people we met seemed gracious and generous, the way people in the Old South always did. Life was quiet and unhurried.

On the other hand, there was this undercurrent of something happening around Falwell, like a dark, subterranean fountain continuously bubbling, with lots of activity, strange people coming and going, rumors of illicit practices, and, over it all, Falwell's growing influence in national politics and religion. He had been in the news during Jimmy Carter's administration for attacking Carter's admission to *Playboy* magazine that he had experienced lust in his heart. He had sued *Penthouse* magazine for $10 million because it published an article based on interviews he had given to freelance reporters. He had made several trips to Israel to visit his friend Menachem Begin, and was spearheading the movement known as Christian Zionism, a name expressing the belief that modern Israel was the fulfillment of biblical "End Times" prophecy. And, as head of the recently formed Moral Majority, he had presided as the host pastor when Ronald Reagan came to Lynchburg on October 3, 1980, to address the National Religious Broadcasters convention that helped put Reagan in the White House a month later.

My wife and I didn't realize it at the time, but we were entering a period that would almost totally alter our understanding of life, faith, and the church.

TWO

Becoming a Theologian

I was theologically naive when I went to Lynchburg in
the late summer of 1980. I had had the requisite training in
theology at Harvard, including a panoply of courses in church
history from the rigorous George Huntston Williams; courses
in Reformation theology with Paul Tillich and Heiko Ober-
man; a couple of Tillich's graduate seminars; and a course in
contemporary theology with Richard R. Niebuhr, the son
of H. Richard Niebuhr of Yale and nephew of the illustrious Reinhold Niebuhr at Union—all of which had allowed
me to easily pass the theology section of the divinity school's
qualifying exams. Later, at Princeton Theological Seminary, I

took a famous seminar in the theology of Karl Barth under the renowned Barthian scholar George S. Hendry. But I simply didn't think theologically. Theology didn't interest me.

For fifteen years at Vanderbilt, I had been professor of preaching, worship, and literature. These were the subjects I had lectured and written about—these and Christian spirituality. As I approached midlife, I became more and more enamored of spirituality, and had written four or five books about prayer and the inner life.

In Lynchburg, I wanted to be a good preacher, to justify what I had been telling my students for years, that the church needed truly good preaching: not just evangelical rhetoric of the kind provided by Billy Graham, but preaching that probed people's minds and hearts, and led them, week by week, to hitch up their lives and become truer, more mature followers of Christ.

My first sermon in Lynchburg was called "Jesus and the Terror of Moving." It began:

> For some weeks now, I have been living under a motto I read on a poster: "Life Is a Moving Experience." I am not, I confess, a good mover. In fact, I am a very poor mover. Moving temporarily destroys me. The uprooting is more than I can bear. Morning after morning, I have awakened before dawn in the cold grip of anxieties, certain that I would not survive the relocation. The last few nights before our move, I took an extra pillow to bed with me. When the anxieties came, I would clutch it the way a child clutches a teddy bear, reverting to some basic need for security. There

is only one word to describe what I was feeling: terror. I was absolutely terrified at the thought of moving.

I shared my feelings of angst at leaving our beautiful home in Nashville and the relaxed, casual nature of my work at Vanderbilt. To make the move was an act of faith, I said, faith that eventually conquered my fear and uneasiness, and I wanted my parishioners to have that kind of faith too. I quoted a card John R. Mott, the famous globe-trotting missionary, always carried in his pocket: "With God, over the ocean; without God, not over the threshold!"

It was the beginning of what I hoped would be years of real pastoral preaching—honest, confessional, steeped in faith, and inspirational. I little dreamed, at the time, that I would ever have anything to do with Jerry Falwell. His world and mine, even though we were now in the same city, seemed to be a universe apart.

Then, in January of 1981, I preached a sermon called "Would Jesus Have Appeared on the *Old-Time Gospel Hour*?" I wasn't trying to attack Falwell. I had no idea he would even hear about my sermon. What I was attempting to do was to get my own congregation's attention in order to say something about being real Christians in the twentieth century.

Yes, I answered my own question, Jesus probably would appear on the *Old-Time Gospel Hour*. He often appeared in places where he was unexpected. But if he did, I said, he would undoubtedly have said some confrontational things to his hosts, as he often did. For example, he might have said: "You appear to be very religious, before your television audience. But, inside, you are rapacious, unconverted wolves, seeking only a greater share of the evangelical TV market, without really caring for the sheep you devour."

Or: "You take money from widows and children, promising the blessings of God; it is the blessings of God you take from them, only to build an empire."

Or: "You talk of legislating morality as if the Father had given you the franchise on morality and you knew precisely what it is. You hypocrites! Have you not heard that it is immoral to decide for others what they shall read and not read?"

But—and this was the reason for the way I framed the sermon—then I turned the situation around on our own congregation, and said, in effect, "What if Jesus were to appear here in our own sanctuary this morning? What hard things would he have to say to us?

"You take great pride in your elegant sanctuary and beautiful windows," I suggested he might say. "Will they save you from the judgment to come?"

And: "You delight in your hymns and creeds and sacraments. But the poor of the world shall rise up and condemn you, because you have not given yourselves to compassion and justice. You are whited sepulchers, glistening on the outside but putrid and stinking with old carcasses on the inside."

And: "You spend hours preparing your faces and bodies to come to the sanctuary of God; you would do well to spend half the time preparing your souls, that you come not as strangers but as true children of the heavenly Father."

I think it was a very biblical kind of sermon, one that rang with the sound of Jesus' own voice and the vocabulary he frequently employed. But almost no one heard the sermon as a stinging indictment of our own shortcomings as individuals and as a church. Instead, they went out whispering about the way I had skewered Falwell and the *Old-Time Gospel Hour*!

And by that afternoon word of the sermon had spread all over Lynchburg, even to Thomas Road Baptist Church, Liberty Baptist College, and the offices of the Moral Majority!

I had a special hotline to everything going on in Lynchburg. His name was Jim Price. Dr. James J. H. Price. Jim, a cherubic-faced, perennially grinning and eminently likable leprechaun of a man, was a professor of religion at Lynchburg College, the local institution Falwell himself had dropped out of, and served as a part-time minister on our staff, where he had once been assistant minister while writing his Ph.D. dissertation. Jim and his colleague William Goodman, also a professor of religion at Lynchburg College and an ordained Presbyterian minister, had assembled a book called *Jerry Falwell: An Unauthorized Profile*. It was a correlation of contrasting statements Falwell had made in different times and places that revealed what an eager, opportunistic preacher he was, willing to say whatever he thought would please the particular audience he was addressing.

For years, Price and Goodman devoted themselves to recording and collecting everything they could by and about Falwell. It was their extracurricular mission as professors of religion. I think for them it amounted almost to a holy calling.

They became the resident experts on their subject. I often said they knew more about Falwell than he did. To him, they were the equivalent of a tin can tied to a dog's tail: he couldn't get away from them! When reporters and journalists came to town and wanted to know anything about Falwell, they went straight to Price and Goodman, who had become a well-known local institution. *The New York Times, The Wall Street Journal, NBC Nightly News, Penthouse* magazine—everybody sought them out.

It was Jim who provided me with a tape recording of Falwell's worship service the Sunday after my sermon on Jesus and the *Old-Time Gospel Hour.* "I don't want you to hurt Dr. Killinger," drawled the familiar voice as he described for his horrified audience how he had been attacked by a fellow clergyman in Lynchburg, "but we don't need him in this town."

It was an ominous warning. Worded as it was, I suspected that it might even be an invitation. And it wasn't long before I realized that I had inadvertently swatted a hornets' nest. Over the next few weeks, my family received several anonymous death threats. "You won't see your father again," a mysterious voice said to one of my sons on the phone.

For a long time after that, I was conscious of shadowy places, and tried to park in the open where I could spot a mugger's approach. I breathed a silent prayer every time I put the key in my car's ignition, half expecting to be blown to kingdom come!

I had never thought about phone taps, or supposed I

might need to think about them at all. But my wife's sister, whose son was a policeman and was more familiar with such things than we were, said to Anne one day on the telephone, "What's that clicking noise on your phone?"

"I don't know," said Anne.

"I do," said her sister, answering her own question. "Your phone is tapped. Somebody's recording our conversation."

Someone let the air out of the tires on our older son's car while he was at work. Another time they smeared cold cream on his car and then threw the bottle against the hood, denting it.

Our trash often disappeared during the night between the time I set it by the road for pickup and the time when the garbage truck arrived the next morning. We could only imagine people sifting through it for "evidence" it might contain, especially anything we wouldn't want people to know about—copies of mail, business receipts, pornographic films or magazines, anything to tarnish our reputation in the community.

When my wife told her friend Judy Hill, who was a medical records professional, Judy said we should plant things in our trash—copies of *Playboy* and *Hustler,* X-rated videos, and trumped-up pages from personal diaries—and wait to see what would happen.

I couldn't believe Falwell and his people were so sensitive. I was only a new minister in town. Compared to him, I was completely unknown. Granted, there were some powerful people in my congregation. But they weren't going to lead an anti-Falwell campaign because of anything I said. If they did anything at all, it would probably be to fire me!

Price and Goodman were privately gleeful. The only other local who had spoken out against Falwell and the *OTGH* in Lynchburg, besides themselves, was another Lynchburg College professor named Jere Real, whose specialty was writing letters to the editors of newspapers in the area. They were eager to follow the development of this new irritant under Falwell's skin.

I have wondered, if Falwell had not responded at all to that initial sermon, whether I would ever have spoken out again about what he and his followers were doing. But I had never shrunk from a fight, even when I was a small, nearsighted boy trying to cope with bullies considerably larger and stronger than I was, and I was not about to shrink from this one.

I had preached "Would Jesus Have Appeared on the *Old-Time Gospel Hour*?" on January 11, 1981. On March 15, 1981, barely two months later, I preached a sermon called "Could Jesus Belong to the Moral Majority?"

It began with an observation from G. K. Chesterton that Saint John in his Apocalypse had beheld many strange and impossible creatures, but none so strange and impossible as some of his own commentators. It was the same for Jesus, I said; his name had been invoked through the ages by many groups and causes to which he would not willingly give it. In my opinion, the Moral Majority was one of these.

It was "palpably ironic," I continued, for Jesus to be

linked with the Moral Majority, because "in his own time he was considered by most religious authorities to be grossly immoral." The scribes and Pharisees accused him of consorting with known sinners, working on the Sabbath, encouraging his disciples to ignore cleanliness laws, usurping the prerogative of God to forgive sins, and blasphemously employing the name of God without specific authority to do so. In short, Jesus was considered a moral outcast by many of his own people.

Jesus was obviously a moral person, I conceded—perhaps the most moral man who ever lived—but he refused to submit his behavior to the legal arbiters of his day. He did not equate morality with spirituality. In fact, he consistently demonstrated that there was a vast difference between the two, and inveighed against confusing them.

I told a story that had meant a great deal to me since hearing it years before when a swarthy little man from Sri Lanka named D. T. Niles had told it during Princeton University's 250th anniversary celebration. It involved a certain Dr. Robert Mackie who, as moderator of the Church of Scotland, was sent with two Plymouth Brethren ministers shortly after World War Two to check on the World Council of Churches' work in Asia Minor. The three men arrived by Jeep at a small Orthodox church in a remote area of Greece, where they were welcomed by a local priest who was overjoyed to see them.

Eager to assure his visitors of his delight in their presence, the priest produced a partial box of Havana cigars a parishioner had given him before the war and he had carefully hoarded for special occasions. Dr. Mackie accepted a cigar, bit the end off, lit it, puffed on it contentedly, and pronounced it an excellent smoke. The Plymouth Brethren were offended. They drew themselves up haughtily and intoned, almost in unison, "No, thank you, we don't smoke!"

Realizing he had offended the two men, and eager to make amends, the poor priest disappeared into the cave below his house and returned with a flagon of his best wine, which he proceeded to offer them.

Dr. Mackie took a glass, sniffed the bouquet of the wine, sipped it, rolled it around on his tongue meditatively, and said how fine it was.

The two Plymouth Brethren, more horrified than ever, shrank visibly from the very idea that they would imbibe alcoholic spirits. "No, thank you," they said even more forcefully than before, "we don't drink!"

Later, as the three men climbed into the Jeep and waved farewell to the priest, the Plymouth Brethren turned on Dr. Mackie with a vengeance. "Dr. Mackie," they said, "do you mean to tell us that you are the moderator of the Church of Scotland and a representative of the World Council of Churches and you both smoke and drink?!"

Dr. Mackie had had more of his priggish companions than he could possibly stand. "No, dammit, I don't," he exploded, "but *somebody* had to be a Christian!"

"It is all right to be opposed to drinking or other forms of drug taking," I said in my sermon; "but let's not confuse that with being Christian. It is all right to be opposed to homosexuality as a lifestyle; but let's not confuse that with being Christian. It is all right to be opposed to corrupt politics; but let's not confuse that with being Christian."

Now, today, I would not say it is all right to be opposed to homosexuality as a lifestyle. I am sorry I said that, for I no longer believe it is excusable behavior to be opposed to anyone on the basis of their sexual preference, even apart from one's religious beliefs.

But the point I went on to make in the sermon was that the church of Jesus Christ must always resist being turned into a center of piety and legalism. "The tragedy for the church, when it becomes identified with morality," I said, "is that it unwittingly broadcasts the opposite of Jesus' message that God receives sinners." To confuse the church with morality is "to establish a new Phariseeism, to enthrone the enemies of Jesus at the center of what we are about."

If Jesus were to show up at a Moral Majority rally—and who is to say he doesn't? I suggested—"the persons he would really identify with would be the ones under attack."

I didn't realize it at the time, but I was beginning to think like a theologian. I wasn't merely a preacher of the Gospel, I wasn't speaking only as a pastor, I was taking on the role of a prophet!

I wasn't like the Reverend Dr. William Dixon Gray, a Presbyterian friend of mine in Nashville who made a trip to Haiti, beheld the desperate hunger among many poor people of that little island, came home, and could never get the subject of hunger out of his sermons again, so that the board of his church asked him to take early retirement and give them a rest from the topic that was devouring him. But as

Falwell and his people continued to fight back and I was pilloried by letters to the editor of the local paper, I determinedly preached occasional sermons about televangelists and their apparent greed for money and power. I felt that it had become a part of my prophetic challenge.

Looking back now at the record of my sermons during my tenure in Lynchburg, I see such titles as "The Gospel for the Tired," "Christmas Is for Simple Folk," "Life's Unfinished Business," "Discovering the Joy of Your Limitations," "What You Are Missing When You Don't Pray," "The Importance of Being Connected," "Success Is a Failure Experience," "The 'Aye' of the Storm," "Being Yourself Before God," and "Living More in a World of Less"—all strongly *pastoral* subjects.

I published, from those six years, several volumes of sermons I had preached as teaching series: *Christ and the Seasons of Marriage; The Cup and the Waterfall* (a series on prayer); *The God Named Hallowed: The Lord's Prayer for Today; To My People with Love: The Ten Commandments for Today; Christmas Parables; Christmas Spoken Here;* and *Sea Breezes: Thoughts of God from a Summer Beach.* And I would later publish two collections of prayers and affirmations, *Lost in Wonder, Love, and Praise* and *Enter Every Trembling Heart,* many of which I had written as worship aids for Sunday services in Lynchburg.

In other words, I wasn't obsessed by Jerry Falwell, the *Old-Time Gospel Hour,* the Moral Majority, and televangelists in general. But I began to realize the importance of local pastors' speaking out on headline subjects of their day, especially those that touched on religion and helped to shape their understanding of God, the church, and the Gospel, and I felt it incumbent upon me, especially because I was speaking from a Lynchburg pulpit, to direct occasional sermons at what I saw plainly as abuses being perpetrated on the Christian religion by prominent voices in the media.

In all, I preached perhaps ten or twelve sermons in six years about the distortions of truth and excesses of misguided zeal I saw around me—sermons with such titles as "What Is Wrong With the TV Evangelists," "The Packaging of the Gospel," "When Religion Makes You Sick," "The Wideness of Christ and the Narrowness of Christianity," "What Must I Do to Be Saved—Intelligently?" "The Real Language of Faith," "The Moral Voice in an Immoral World," and "The Day the Moral Majority Went Home."

And I preached a series of sermons on reading the Bible: "Did God Write the Bible?" "Did Jesus Believe in the Inerrancy of Scripture?" "The Bible and Modern Science," "The Humor of the Bible," and "The Bible and the End of the World."

I took preaching very seriously. I had once written a book called *The Centrality of Preaching in the Total Task of the Ministry*, and I believed that preaching *is* truly central to what a minister does, especially if the minister has any talent to interpret Scripture and understand how it relates to people's lives in the contemporary situation. In my case, I felt a compulsion—a calling, even—to preach *correctively,* trying to balance what preachers such as Falwell and Pat Robertson and Jim Bakker were declaring to be the outlines of faith.

I look back at my six years in the Lynchburg pulpit now and realize how my presence there, across town from Jerry Falwell and contending with Falwell over numerous issues about which he loved to make blithe and often erroneous comments, actually did transform me from a mere preacher when I arrived into a more-or-less-seasoned theologian when I left. It wasn't a conscious thing. I didn't wake up one day and say, "I had better become a theologian in order to counteract Mr. Falwell." I simply elided into thinking and preaching theologically, into always measuring what I said by my newly developing standards, by the outline of theological understanding that was constantly growing inside me.

To the extent that I am a theologian, and can call myself one today, it is owing to Jerry Falwell and the necessity of speaking out on topic after topic as he sent them spiraling up from his pulpit at Thomas Road Baptist Church. I no longer had the luxury of dealing only with questions of spirituality and what makes a Christian in general. I had to consider what makes a Christian under particular circumstances, when dealing with politics, abortion, homosexuality, poverty, materialism, greed, other religions, and whatever else confronts us in the modern world.

The same thing happened, I am convinced, to John Shelby Spong. Spong was minister of St. John's Episcopal Church in Lynchburg from 1965 to 1969. St. John's stood just off Rivermont Avenue about halfway between First Presbyterian Church and downtown, close to Randolph-Macon College, and had perhaps a quarter of the city's wealthier, more illustrious citizens in it. It was a conservative, laissez-faire church that, like most Episcopal congregations at the end of the war in Vietnam, appeared to be more interested in the taste of Earl Grey tea and the price of stocks than it did in radical Christianity. It was an unlikely pastorate for a man who would later become a rabble-rousing bishop noted as a critic of fundamentalism and a minister to homosexuals.

Spong has described on his Web site what a circus he found taking place across town at Thomas Road Baptist Church: "One week, Miss America would be present in swim suit and gown to give her witness, the next week it would be the Chaplain of Bourbon Street. It was not unlike 'marrying Sam,' the preacher in Al Capp's comic strip 'L'il Abner,' who offered to wrestle a bear for a higher wedding fee."

Spong tells in his autobiography, *Here I Stand* (an identification with Luther's *Hier stehe ich, ich kann nicht anders*—"Here I stand, I cannot do otherwise"), about his almost visceral reaction to such hijinks and how he began, even then, to rethink what church and Christianity are really about. When we consider the titles of some of his later books— *Rescuing the Bible from Fundamentalism, Human Sexuality, Why Christianity Must Change or Die*—it becomes obvious that what was going on across town in Falwell's church had already fired his imagination as a preacher of truth and righteousness. Becoming a bishop gave him a platform for mounting a campaign against the ignorance, reactionism, and irresponsibility not only in his own church but in America's religion as a whole.

First Presbyterian was a lot like St. John's, only more so. If St. John's had a quarter of the wealthy, influential citizens of Lynchburg, First Presbyterian had half of them, and its buildings, erected on a large, tree-studded campus with the Blue Ridge Mountains for a backdrop, were more elegant and spacious than St. John's. Its parishioners, moreover, lay clustered around its nearby neighborhoods like a bivouacked army, in mostly elegant, beautiful old homes. I don't remember all the statistics, but I do recall that there were sixty-five medical doctors in the membership at one count, and an equal number of lawyers, teachers, bankers, and business leaders. Not all the doctors were in church every Sunday, of course. But there were enough that when Claggett Jones, a beloved little man in his late seventies, had a heart attack during a morning service, so many physicians clustered around him in a matter of seconds that someone had to order them to stand back and give him air!

This congregation, like the one at St. John's, was upper middle class and prided itself on its cosmopolitanism and savoir faire. Its beautiful sanctuary boasted the finest stained-glass windows in town, and its music program, under the direction of a British organist named Norman Blake, who had developed his skill at improvisationalism while playing for silent films, was considered the best in the state. As was the case at St. John's, the congregation's leaders were generally more concerned about the sanctuary's acoustics and the dignity of the choir robes than they were about poverty, segregation, or many other social problems.

One of my predecessors twice removed, Dr. Herbert

Barks, told us two stories that said volumes about the church.

The first was about the color of his shoes. Brought to Lynchburg from Glendale, California, after a nationwide search, Herb was a youngish, fairly casual minister. The first Sunday after he arrived in Lynchburg, he wore brown shoes with a dark suit hidden by his pulpit robe. Immediately after the service, he was waited upon by two of the more powerful women of the congregation, who informed him that the minister of their church always wore *black* shoes in the pulpit on Sunday.

Herb got the message, and from then on wore only black shoes—until his final Sunday at the church. On that Sunday, he processed down the aisle behind the choir at the eleven o'clock service wearing a pair of white tennis shoes!

The other story was about a session meeting (the session is the main board of elders in the Presbyterian Church) that was going on during a particularly hairy season in the town when crosses had been burned on the lawn of the church because Herb was known to sympathize with Martin Luther King, Jr., and the integration movement. A man named Charlie Leys, who was an employee of the Leggett Department Stores, had been dispatched to the meeting that evening with instructions from Mrs. Leggett, who was also a member of the church, to advance a motion that in the future only sheep manure would be used on the church's extensive rose gardens, as she was convinced that cow manure was not good for roses.

Another member of the board—Herb could not recall his

name—was an avid gardener and insisted that cow manure *was* good for roses but sheep manure was not. A big debate followed, and for more than an hour the session occupied itself with trying to decide whether or not to honor Mrs. Leggett's request.

At the end of an hour, Bruce Thomson, who was president of a three-state Coca-Cola bottling plant and an old farmboy himself, forgot to say "manure" and used a more earthy Anglo-Saxon term.

From then on, it was "cow shit" this and "sheep shit" that for another forty-five minutes, until everyone was exhausted and the conversation suddenly languished for want of fresh fuel.

I have already mentioned George Stewart, president of the First Colony Life Insurance Company. At this point in time, the session of First Presbyterian Church, as, indeed, of most Presbyterian churches in that era, was still exclusively male, and it was almost as exclusively composed of native Lynchburgers, there being in general a deep distrust of outsiders. George Stewart was the single exception to this unspoken rule. As one of the town's wealthier citizens and probably its biggest mover-and-shaker, he had been installed as the very first elder who did not qualify as an old Lynchburger.

George had been sitting quietly at one end of the boardroom table, opposite the minister and the clerk of session. Now, when the room fell unexpectedly quiet, George spoke. "Boys," he said in a quiet, apparently sincere manner, "I'd like to say a good word for bullshit!"

For a split second, nobody made a sound. Then the entire room erupted in raucous laughter.

"When it died down," said Herb, "we had a prayer and went home."

That was Lynchburg in a nutshell. Cities all over the United States were burning down with angry demonstrations. Jerry Falwell and the *Lynchburg News and Advance* claimed it was all inspired by communists. Falwell said that Nelson Mandela was a troublemaker and belonged in jail. His church's private school was openly advertised as being for whites only. And the most prestigious church in Lynchburg was having an argument about what kind of manure to spread on its rose beds!

For any pastor from the outside world, like Herb Barks or John Shelby Spong or myself, it was a surreal place to be. The absurdities and anomalies of life in that little city, isolated from the mainstream of American culture, were enough to make us question our sanity. I had once written a book about the theater of the absurd, and moving to Lynchburg made me feel as if I had stepped onto the stage in one of its crazy, offbeat plays.

Some nights, when I wasn't too tired, I lay awake in the dark and thought about it. I thought about Nashville, the lively, progressive city from which we had come, and Vanderbilt Divinity School with its frontline programs and cutting-edge lecturers. And then I thought about this trivial little town still locked in its mid-nineteenth-century ways, and Jerry Falwell, who was flying all over kingdom come, beating the drum for fundamentalists and evangelicals to take over the nation, and I wanted to say, "God, why? Why me, in this place, at this time? What have I done so awful that I deserve to spend whole years of my life, the only life I have, in Lynchburg, Virginia?"

THREE

Touching a Nerve

I had preached my first sermon that attracted Falwell's attention—"Would Jesus Have Appeared on the *Old-Time Gospel Hour?*"—on January 11, 1981. Falwell was riding high then, stopping by the White House practically at will, commanding vast troops of conservatives all over the United States, and saying outrageous things about communism and homosexuals and racial integration and the women's movement that were instantly picked up by the media and repeated in sermons from a thousand pulpits. We were getting death threats and having our phone tapped, but nobody really paid much attention to the unequal quarrel in which he and I were engaged.

Suddenly caught up in this new situation, I began to be aware of all the other voices clamoring for attention on the religious scene.

There was Pat Robertson, Falwell's closest neighbor, whose Christian Broadcasting Network and *700 Club,* named for his seven hundred original and continuing donors, were reaching millions of viewers. Robertson had poured his effort into creating a law school and recruiting and training media journalists. He would one day make a bid for the U.S. presidency, and the right-wing tenor of his Regents University would one day make headline news when Monica Goodling was called to testify before the Senate about her role in recruiting Republican attorneys for the Justice Department.

There were Jim and Tammy Bakker, the incredibly naive, wide-eyed, gamin-like stars of the *PTL Club* (for "Praise the Lord") in Charlotte, North Carolina, who ran their charismatic ministry like a game-show circus, with incredible cockamamie attractions designed to draw and entertain an audience, and to enlist their donations to build a luxurious retirement and amusement center at Fort Mill, South Carolina, called Heritage U.S.A. I happened to see their program the day they had a praying elephant on it and were taking phone requests for special prayers. Bakker would later be indicted for fraud and sent to jail for overselling timeshares in his village.

There was Jimmy Swaggart, the talented, good-looking Pentecostalist preacher who was caught visiting a prostitute, then wept and whined his way back to acceptance by his supporters. A cousin of Jerry Lee Lewis, Swaggart loved to sit at the piano and play frantic, jazzed-up renditions of old hymns, then leap up to croon a seductive invitation for donations that would result in people's receiving the blessings God wanted to send them.

There were Bob Tilton, the Texas evangelist who was filmed sitting in a rowboat on a lake praying for people, scrunching up his eyes as he ejaculated the word "Amen!" at the end of every petition, and James Robison, another charismatic Texan, who dramatized his contempt for secular culture, and somehow, thereby, his faith in the biblical God, by viciously slashing a valuable classical painting in front of the cameras.

There was Oral Roberts, the Pentecostalist evangelist who parlayed his Holy Ghost ministry into a famous university, seminary, and medical school in Tulsa that bragged of being the first totally computerized campus in the United States. At one point, Oral claimed that God said he was going to kill him if viewers didn't send $8 million needed to keep his ministry afloat. He got the money, but his reputation was damaged by a former associate who told how the thousands of prayer requests that came in weekly were hauled off to be burned and not personally carried by Oral, per his faithful promise, into the famous tower topped by gigantic praying hands.

There was Robert Schuller, the monkey-faced, saccharinely dramatic dean of the Crystal Cathedral in Orange County, California, whose *Hour of Power* was one of the classiest religious programs on television, complete with testimonies from Hollywood stars reportedly paid as much as $50,000 each for their appearances. Schuller himself maintained expensive homes in Hawaii and Colorado, as well as one in Orange County, but his organization was often months behind with employees' salaries. I didn't find Schuller as personally offensive as most of the other TV preachers, but the stories I heard from inside his organization when I lived in Los Angeles were enough to validate his inclusion on a list with the rest of them.

The religious culture of America was filled with these audacious, narcissistic, self-serving priests of the airwaves, who were forever hawking books and gewgaws and keeping vast teams of employees at work opening people's gifts, recording addresses into donor rolls, and sending out SOS's requesting more and more money to keep them from "going under." Jerry Falwell, according to one of his lieutenants, claimed credit for "inventing" the emergency-fund request to keep his ministry afloat, and it became a staple of all the unconscionable media preachers with their insatiable appetites for bigger campuses, more extensive media coverage, and personal celebrityhood.

Typical of the begging letters sent out to gullible Christians all over America was this one mailed out by Falwell on April 30, 1981:

> It now appears that, after 25 years of broadcasting and televising the Gospel, the Old-Time Gospel Hour may go off the air. . . . It breaks my heart to tell you this. But, it is the

truth. The Old-Time Gospel Hour simply cannot continue
with a 60 to 90 day deficit—especially when that deficit is
increasing. . . . If we are unable to pay off this deficit in the
next few days, we simply must cancel our programs. . . . I
must be absolutely honest with you; our situation is now at
the crisis stage.

An entire subculture of ministry workers emerged in TV
evangelism, with dossiers showing who they had worked for
and what successful fund-raisers they had been, and these
people circulated constantly among the major evangelistic
headquarters like sharks in search of better feeding grounds.

Somebody, I thought, ought to nail these moguls of religious sleaze for who they really were and what their organizations were like. Most of the media treated them like celebrities
and nobody appeared to be dealing with the incalculable dam-
age they were doing to honest religion. It was as if they had
bound and gagged genuine Christianity, dumped it in a
closet, then impersonated it and made obscene profits out of
the switch.

I was constantly learning more about Falwell's operation
and knew it was essentially the same with all the other big-
time evangelists. My informants from Liberty Baptist College were painting a dreadful picture of that "wonderful
Christian institution," as Falwell bragged about it on TV. In
fact, it was totally riddled with hypocrisy. Falwell and his
lieutenants, most of whom had honorary D.D.'s purchased
from diploma mills or awarded by little fundamentalist colleges, were jealous of the real Ph.D.'s on the faculty, and

were always taking potshots at them for being "intellectu-als" or "jerks."

At the same time that Falwell claimed to be building "a great Christian university," speakers in Liberty Baptist College's chapel warned students against reading books or going to art galleries because there was nothing in them worth knowing about. Ministerial students who cut classes commonly gave their professors the excuse that they had become so caught up in their devotions, and God was blessing them so fiercely, that they had forgotten everything, including their responsibility to attend class.

Sexual repression on the Liberty campus resulted in an atmosphere of perverted sensuality. Girls wore long skirts but favored the ones with slits up the side because they knew they were provocative. Boys were urged to confess that they had lusted or masturbated. One professor of evangelism was described as having his huge class—more than five hundred students—bow their heads in prayer, and during the prayer, raise their hands. "Now," he intoned, "if you are masturbating, wiggle one finger." As dozens of students came under conviction and wiggled their fingers, he had prayer for them and talked luridly about how sex would ruin their lives.

Many students refused to take this professor's classes a second or third time because they said he was embarrassingly fixated on sex.

The emphasis on sports at Liberty was as strong as if it had been a Big Ten university. Falwell confessed publicly that he was "a sports nut." The urge to win trumped everything else. Some coaches resigned because the administration put so much pressure on them to produce winning teams. On one hand, they were expected to spend time with their families, but on the other hand they were constantly prodded to get the college into Class A competitions.

Racial and sexual prejudice were rife. Students were told that Martin Luther King, Jr., was a devil and women were inferior to men. The few blacks on campus were openly snubbed by other students. Girls seldom spoke in classes. Falwell publicly called homosexuals "kooks," and the slightest hint that a student was homosexual led to immediate expulsion. Religious charismatics were frowned on, even though Falwell said publicly that they were as good as other Christians. Faculty were told they could only attend Thomas Road Baptist Church. Many of them privately admitted that they couldn't get their Christianity disentangled from the banks of TV lights and cameras in the sanctuary of Thomas Road Baptist Church.

Similar tales were emanating from the churches and schools of other TV evangelists. The whole, basically anticultural religious movement was spreading like a mucky fungus across American Christianity and I felt the need to speak out about it. Teaching in a liberal divinity school for fifteen years, I hadn't really been paying attention to it. Now, living in the same town with the most egregious example of the fungus, I felt a responsibility to sound the alarm.

It wasn't in my nature. I wasn't a combative person. Actually I was a mystic who craved solitude and quietness above everything else. But, for God's sake, somebody had to talk about it!

So, on August 30, 1981, barely six months after I had in-advertently become Falwell's enemy by preaching "Would Jesus Have Appeared on the *Old-Time Gospel Hour?*" I preached a sermon called "What Is Wrong with the TV Evangelists."

My text was John 10:11–13, where Jesus talked about "hireling shepherds," shepherds who undertook the super-intendence of flocks not for the care and protection of their sheep but in order to fleece them, to make a profit from their office.

It didn't take me long to move from talking about televi-sion's power for good and evil to addressing the problems I saw in the major media evangelists of the last five years:

"They are shallow and ahistorical," I said. "None of them has been deeply rooted either in the traditions of a great church or in the tenets of a great theological position. They are like waterbugs skating on the surface of the pond, with little or no acquaintance in ecclesiastical or theological depths."

I was not an academic snob, and didn't insist that there could not be great ministers who hadn't attended good uni-versities and seminaries. But it did seem to me that most of the evangelistic prima donnas currently exhorting the masses via TV were "singularly unprepared by education to give in-struction in matters spiritual or theological."

They were clever enough—certainly some of them might have earned Ph.D.'s in cleverness. But Sinclair Lewis's fictional character Elmer Gantry, the very model of an ambitious, self-serving minister, was clever too, even though he had been a mediocre student in seminary.

My second observation was that the majority of TV evangelists were "hopelessly self-centered and opportunistic" people whose greatest concern was M-O-N-E-Y, "the voracious Gog and Magog of their industry," and not the many "causes" they were always espousing. I didn't name Falwell, but I did refer to an evangelist whose ministry pled for large gifts to rescue and resettle the boat people of South Vietnam, then used only a fraction of the money that was donated actually to relieve any of those for whom the gifts were designated.

I described how typical evangelists' mail was handled, with assembly lines of people opening envelopes, separating checks from letters, and entering codes on the letters about which of their computerized messages would best respond to the senders' messages. The computers, of course, checked their own memory banks to be certain the same messages had not been sent before, then printed the designated messages and signed the evangelist's name.

From then on, the senders could be assured of receiving a constant stream of mail from the evangelist. Friends in Lynchburg once sent the name of a family cat to the *Old-Time Gospel Hour,* and for years the cat received mail from *OTGH.* I called it "one of the greatest con games in the history of America," and one the FCC never interfered with because of the much-abused principle known as the separation of church and state.

"The ultimate problem" with the TV evangelists, I went on to say, "is that the message and methods of these evangelists create among millions of people a false impression of what true Christianity is."

TV Christianity completely ignored the deeply communal nature of salvation, which always required assembling with other Christians, observing the Lord's Supper, and sharing the Lord's love with one another. Instead, TV Christianity was "a consumer-based religion . . . calculated to appeal to the self-pandering instincts of every viewer for the absolution of private sin and the dispatching of personal illness or problems." It created a completely false impression of what following Christ is all about.

"TV Christianity promises rose-scented pathways to heaven," I said; "real Christianity offers a crown of thorns and death with our Lord."

Because this misrepresentation was so misleading and pernicious, I argued, people should withhold their funds and put TV Christianity out of existence before it totally corrupted the religious instincts off of which it fed. The good it pretended to do was completely illusory and nonexistent; it was a fabrication of the evangelists themselves, who were utterly without scruples, like the most avaricious used-car salesmen in America.

Of course they made their ministries look successful, and that in itself bamboozled many well-meaning people of true devotion into believing they were sincere and trustworthy. But TV Christianity was wrong, and people needed to know it was wrong.

"A few months ago," I said, "I was interviewed by an NBC newscaster. At the end of a long conversation, he asked a question designed to sum up everything. 'If you could say one thing to the followers of [a certain evangelist],' he said, 'what would it be?' My answer was rambling and ineffective, because I was secretly biting my tongue to keep from giving the reply that leapt immediately to mind, but which I was sure would be vastly offensive to many of those who would hear it. What I wanted to say but didn't was: 'Don't drink any Kool-Aid!' I wanted instinctively to say that, because people are so often like the poor sheep who followed the insane founder of Jonestown, and because the shepherds are so often hirelings who care nothing for the sheep.

"And Jesus, who died for the sheep, doesn't like them to be misled!"

I had compared the response to my first sermon, "Would Jesus Have Appeared on the *Old-Time Gospel Hour?*" to what Martin Luther said happened after he posted his ninety-five theses on the chapel door at Wittenberg and Karl Barth said resulted from the publication of his book on Paul's Letter to the Romans, *Der Römerbrief*—I felt as if I had been sleepwalking, had somehow got hold of the bell rope in the church tower, and had inadvertently awakened the whole town!

But the response to that sermon was small compared to what followed in the wake of this sermon. Part of the reason was that the sermon began to be quoted everywhere, in the *Richmond Times-Dispatch, The New York Times, The Los Angeles Times,* even the *International Herald Tribune.* Segments of it were read on radio stations all over the United States and Canada. One magazine called *Spotlight* apparently had a very wide audience, because the publication of my sermon prompted mail from virtually everywhere—Florida, Vermont, New York, California, Montana, even France and Spain.

A few letters expressed gratitude that someone had at last contested the media evangelists and the kind of unhealthy religion they represented. "You are beautiful and brave," wrote one woman, "thank you for speaking out."

"You are to be commended in the highest possible terms," said another, "for your timely and eloquent remarks concerning television evangelists."

A Roman Catholic priest wrote: "I support your position fully."

Of all my mail, I think the letter I appreciated most was a three-page, handwritten missive scrawled by Dr. Gordon Poteat, a retired scholar living in Ormond Beach, Florida. His wife had read my sermon to him, he said, because he could no longer see to do it himself. "If you have read my exposition of James in *The Interpreter's Bible,*" he said in his final paragraph, "you will know we are on the same wavelength."

But negative responses far outnumbered positive ones. Many appeared to have been written by senior citizens who were faithfully sending their money to the evangelists and believed them to be both sincere and helpful. One lady from Atascadero, California, addressed her letter "To a Dr. John Killinger that doesn't know the meaning of Christian!"

"I'm amazed," she wrote, "that you a Christian minister (if you are) that you would run down publicly a brother in Christ. I'll bet you don't even believe in the 'Virgin Birth' or that Jesus Christ is God!"

My "blasting" a Christian pastor "doing so much for families and our country," she said, made her "sick at heart."

"Believe me," she concluded her letter, "I'd sure hate to be in [your] shoes at the time you stand before 'God' and he ask[s] you why you delighted in 'persecution' of another Christian pastor in your own town. *Pride, pride, pride,* that's what God calls it."

She signed her letter: "In Christian Love to Dr. Killinger but not his sinful ways."

"I have just read your views on T.V. evangelists," said a woman in Rochester, New York, "and feeling sorry for you I thought I'd write. T.V. evangelists are *wonderful.* P.T.L.—the 700 Club—Jimmy Swaggart and Ken Copeland—and Oral Roberts—all filled with the spirit of the Lord. They are teaching the *truth* of the Lord and bringing people out of *dead* churches. [God] heals us and answers our prayers. And when I give to the Lord it comes back—10 or 100 fold. I'll pray for you—you need it."

Someone in Austin, Kentucky (I couldn't tell from the signature if it was a man or a woman), wrote: "[Your criticism of Jerry Falwell] simply made my blood boil to think that you would do a thing like that to a fellow pastor publically [*sic*] and to his back. You do this at a time when Jerry Falwell, James Robinson [*sic*], Bob Jones, Jimmy Swagart [*sic*], Rex Humbard, Larry Jones, Oral Roberts and many others are doing a tremendous job turning thousands back to Christ. . . . I am happy to send the above evangelists money every month. They can reach millions of people by television where you reach possibly a few hundred at the most. . . . [They] are trying their very best to convince young and old that abortion, pornography, homes falling apart and many other things including corruption in our government is wrong and destroying mankind and our American way of life."

I was astonished at the viciousness of many of the letters. People said God hated me and they hoped he would get me, then signed their letters "In Christian love." Others said I should beware of walking down any dark streets at night or eating anything in a public place. Still others said they looked forward to someday watching from heaven and seeing me writhing in hell.

Jim Price shared with me the priceless letter he received from an anonymous writer, a woman, who signed herself "A Reader of Globe." She called Jim "an impostor," "one of Satan's angels," and "a Pharisee." She said Jim would one day be in hell and would "look up to the throne of God and see Jerry Falwell." She said she contributed to Falwell monthly, and that Jim was jealous because he couldn't hold a candle to her idol.

She concluded her letter by announcing, "I always pray that the Russian leaders will have poor health, and that is what I am going to pray for you."

On the whole, I could divide the letters I received into two groups: those from educated writers, who expressed themselves well, and those from the less educated, whose expressions were frequently ungrammatical though sometimes colorful. The educated ones were almost always supportive of what I had said and the others were invariably against it.

Reading the letters today, I can see that Falwell and the other TV evangelists were appealing to one of two segments in society that was generally angry or unhappy with the other segment and were already helping that segment to define and express itself against the other. In other words, they were already exploiting and encouraging a division in American society that would become deeper and wider, finding its political fulfillment in the election of George W. Bush in 2000 and 2004.

Falwell and Robertson did more to orchestrate this division than the other televangelists because they used demagoguery to achieve their goals. Falwell in particular employed paranoia as a constant technique for identifying his followers and coaxing them toward cohesion. He often "warned" his audiences at Thomas Road Baptist Church and on the *Old-Time Gospel Hour* that his enemies were out to get him and hurt the movement. He painted a picture of them as a beleaguered people in a hostile environment.

For example, on December 13, 1981, during Falwell's informal remarks to the congregation, he was rambling on about the ACLU's involvement in a local nativity-scene controversy, referring to the ACLU lawyers as "buzzards" and saying it was "time to back that bunch of buzzards down." The ACLU was one of his favorite whipping boys, along with communism, secular humanism, and homosexuality.

After he had ranted for a minute or so about this matter, he said:

"Ah, boy, people hate. You know, we got a call this morning. We get two or three hundred letters a month from people who are going to snuff me out and going to hurt my family. This morning we got a call from somebody they [his security people] took very seriously. He called here about 7:30 or 8 o'clock this morning, saying that today they were going to kill me and my family. . . . It's a shame you can't go to church without your family having to have some security officers standing around them to keep them alive in a church service.

"Well, why is the other side so furious [at me] for saying the things I do? Because we are suddenly getting the attention of the American people and this old country is about to turn around—and it needs to turn around—and I think they think they are losing. And I think they're right, they're losing!

(*Long applause from congregation*)

"You know, back when we were losing, we never talked about shooting anybody. We just worked harder. Now we're beginning to win and they want to shoot everybody. I'm glad the American people are just too smart to be sucked into that and we believe God is going to take care of us. And if you happen to see a kook around here who's trying to do something, get him on his knees, lead him to Christ. Take his gun away from him first! (*Laughter*) All right, all right. Ushers, will you come?"

Falwell regularly worked me over in his services. He complained about "a certain preacher" in another part of town who liked to pick on him because he was a true preacher of the Gospel. "Reverend Killinger," he liked to remind his people, "has never been at Thomas Road Baptist Church—never been inside our doors," yet I chose to ridicule and criticize his ministry. Several times he accused me of being "just downright jealous" of him.

"I love him," he protested. "I trust that God will just really move on him for trying to separate the people of God."

He told his people that I portrayed them as "simplistic," "not mainline," and "oddballs." Then he would say, "You know, there are 60 million people in America just like us, who believe in the inerrancy of the Scriptures, who believe in the Holy Bible, and how can he say they are oddballs? Billy Graham and I and Charles Stanley, we're not oddballs. He doesn't know what he's talking about!"

One Sunday morning he spent a quarter of an hour rambling about his enemies. A reporter from *Penthouse* magazine was in town, he said, trying to gather material about him. The reporter had gone to his old high school and tried to get his student record, but the superintendent, who was a friend of his, wouldn't let him have it. Then he had gone snooping around Wiley & Wilson, the contractors who were building Liberty Baptist College, and asked them a lot of questions.

"I just want you to know," said Falwell, "that I love Lynchburg, I love this town so much that I'd never betray anything about this city to *Penthouse* magazine."

"I guess you saw the newspaper this morning," he said. "I didn't read the newspaper, I was reading my Bible this morning. But somebody handed me this article from the newspaper in which Rev. John Killinger made some critical statements about me and this congregation. He said you're simplistic and you're not mainline. I want you to know you're oddballs. (*Laughter*) Rev. George Bean too, over at St. John's Episcopal Church, he criticized us too."

Many of the members at First Presbyterian Church and St. John's Episcopal Church, he declared, "are friends of mine—people who support us—some of them heavily." These are good folks, he said, and they are "not responsible for what their pastors say."

The person who had shown him the newspaper article—apparently a reporter—had asked him what his response to it was. "I'll tell you my response," he said. "It was this. Jesus said to pray for those who despitefully use you.

"I wish they'd call me and say let's have a cup of coffee," he continued, "and we could talk about the things they don't like. But they never do. One thing you'll never hear, folks. You'll never hear Jerry Falwell criticize another servant of God. They think we're oddballs, fanatics, holier-than-thou. They think we're wacky because we believe the Bible. Let's pray for Rev. Killinger and Rev. Bean."

After a fifteen-minute discursion about *Penthouse* and John Killinger and George Bean, Falwell had the audacity to say to his congregation, "I've never taken sermon time away from talking about Jesus to talk about other preachers." And finally, having said this, he turned to Pierre Guillermin, the president of Liberty Baptist College, and asked him to "come and lead us in prayer for these pastors."

This was vintage Falwell, threatening, pretending to be threatened, skillfully circling the wagons for the simple, honest, religious people of the nation against the invaders, the predators, the destroyers of America and the American way of life. I found it ironic that my family and I had received death threats because I spoke out against Falwell, and here he was whipping up sympathy for himself and his cause by talking about how other preachers were criticizing them and how many death threats he received every month. He was truly masterful at playing on people's natural fears to make them believe their way of life was threatened by others and that they needed to make common cause with him against their enemies.

Reflecting on Falwell's style after his death, Bob Felton said on *Blogcritics Magazine*'s "BC Culture" that he had "a sort of blustery, Boss Hogg presence and could play the poor-pitiful-beleaguered-by-Satan-me routine better than almost anybody."

A number of people in my church were unhappy because their minister was making waves for Falwell and the other evangelists. Like most Christians in America, they had an innate reverence for ministers, whatever their particular theological or homiletical idiosyncrasies, and this made them feel awkward when their friends asked them why their pastor seemed to have a vendetta against TV preachers. Few said anything directly to me about this, but I was aware, from bits of conversation I overheard and a few things people did say to my face, that my occasional sermons about TV evangelism were causing them some consternation.

One of my fine, extraordinarily decent deacons apparently believed that I was uninformed about all the good being done by Pat Robertson and his Christian Broadcasting Network. Tom Kirkpatrick was a gentle, soft-spoken contractor in his late fifties or early sixties, and an original member of the *700 Club*. Tom didn't upbraid me for my sermon "What Is Wrong with TV Evangelists." He didn't even mention it to me. But shortly after I preached it, he asked, in his quiet way, if he could take me down to Robertson's headquarters for a special tour. He'd like me to see the operation firsthand, he said.

We rode down to Virginia Beach in Tom's Cadillac, accompanied by a friend of Tom's who, I believe, was also a member of the club. Tom usually drove a pickup truck, and it seemed strange to see him sitting behind the wheel of this big, comfortable car.

We were promptly met on arrival by a very polite man who ushered us into the office of Tucker Yates, vice president of CBN. Yates apologized that Pat Robertson was away and he would be giving us the tour. He was a pleasant, efficient-looking man in early middle age, and spoke in a relaxed way as he conducted us around the studios.

I was impressed, at the time, by the spaciousness of the quarters and the understated elegance of the appointments. There weren't a lot of people bustling around, as I had expected, and the ones who were there didn't appear to be overly busy. In fact, my primary recollection after all these years is of a certain dreamlike quality to the visit, as if we were floating effortlessly through the hallways and studios.

Yates talked sketchily about the number of hours CBN's programs were on the air and how many people they were reaching in this country and that. There were frequent mentions of money, and how much it took to run an operation like this, and it was obvious that donors like Tom and his friend were held in respect by the organization, but I didn't get the feeling that Yates was making a conscious pitch for gifts.

The one thing that seemed to be missing in the whole tour was any sense of how vital to them this business was as a Christian outreach. We might have been touring a secular broadcasting outfit or publishing house, for all the emphasis there was on reaching the lost or providing help for the poor. And Yates unwittingly provided the most memorable moment of the visit by casually describing a recent attempt CBN had made to adjust its programming to reach a wider audience.

We were standing behind a glass, watching a broadcast of the *700 Club* currently in progress. The handsome, soft-spoken African-American cohost, whose name eludes me now, was sitting in for Pat Robertson, who in those days did many of the interviews and commentaries himself. The cohost had temporarily paused to bow his head and offer a prayer.

Yates chuckled. I asked what he was laughing about.

"Oh, nothing," he said, as if brushing off the question. Then he answered. "I was just thinking," he said, "about an effort we made a few weeks ago to revise our format. We wanted to reach out to a larger audience, you know, sort of secularize the program. So we figured we'd make the first part of the program a little less Christian, maybe not have prayers in it, and talk about world news and so forth, then return to our regular format in the second half, after we'd won a few new viewers."

He smiled and chuckled to himself again.

"To show you how far we had gone," he said, "Pat [Robertson] came in one day after a program, slapped his forehead, and said, 'You know what? We didn't pray a single time on the show today!'"

"Did your viewers complain?" I asked.

"Did they!" said Yates. "And how! We really heard about it at our next Founders Club meeting. Several of the guys came armed for bear, and that was all they could talk about. Some of them were even standing in their chairs yelling at us. We had to go back to our old format, the one you're seeing now."

We didn't talk much about the visit as we drove back to Lynchburg that day. I wondered if Tom and his friend had been disappointed at what they had seen. Tom never mentioned the *700 Club* to me again. A couple of years later, he sold his construction company and retired. Then he got involved in our church's work with a new regional food bank program to feed the poor. Every day, regular as clockwork, he drove his truck all over town, collecting donations for the program.

I have a smile on my face as I think about him. He was a lovely man, and a gentle, sincere Christian.

I didn't get to meet Pat Robertson, but I think my visit to the Christian Broadcasting Network only confirmed what I was beginning to understand about all the TV evangelists. Most of them didn't believe all the things they boasted about believing. They knew what many of their followers believed, and they were careful to sound as if they believed those things too. They weren't exactly insincere, but being able to lead their followers sometimes took priority over voicing any private thoughts they might have had.

Maybe I was too uncompromising, and that was what was driving me to speak out against this new, conservative form of Christianity so rampant in America. But I was really worried about the changes taking place in America's religious patterns and what it meant to the mainline churches. Maybe the old churches hadn't represented Christ the way they should have, but at least they didn't thrive on preaching hatred and division the way the evangelicals and fundamentalists did.

I hadn't meant to start a war with Falwell and the other evangelists, but it must have looked to outsiders as if I had. Not long after the sermon about TV evangelists, I began to be besieged by media journalists eager to expand on the story about a minister in Falwell's hometown who disagreed with his message and the methods used to promote it. I was on *NBC Nightly News* with Douglas Kiker and made a lengthy appearance on an episode of the *David Frost Show,* which, as far as I know, was never released in this country. Frost himself didn't come for the interview. It was shot in Lynchburg with a stand-in, and I was told that Frost would take the stand-in's place when the final show was cut in London, personally asking the questions put to me by his substitute.

People magazine came to Lynchburg and photographed me in front of the First Presbyterian Church for a big spread under the headline "His Critics Speak Out and Jerry Falwell's Home Base Becomes a Flock Divided." There was a big photo of me on the page opposite one of Falwell, and a quotation from one of my sermons. The article mentioned James J. H. Price and William Goodman, and their book *Jerry Falwell: An Unauthorized Profile,* and quoted them as saying that Falwell's sermons over a fifteen-year period showed "a pattern of racism, anti-Semitism and general intolerance in the independent Baptist minister's gospel."

The article also quoted Dr. Edward Hindson, one of Falwell's assistant pastors, as dismissing Price and Goodman in a sermon as "not worth shooting. You couldn't find professional killers who would hire on for the price those guys are worth." And it cited a security guard at Liberty Baptist College as saying, "No one ever defies Dr. Falwell and lives."

It was curious, I thought, that a national magazine should set a tone of foreboding in describing the opposition of

three people to the obvious power and success of Falwell
and his organization. Was it only a coincidence or did the
reporters do it intentionally?

None of the reporters ever picked up on another voice
in Lynchburg during those days, but it was a voice I found
especially upsetting.

Dr. Eberhard Bethge, a German pastor and theologian
who had been imprisoned by the Nazis after the failed attempt to kill Adolph Hitler with a bomb, had become a
noted figure in Europe and Great Britain since World War
Two. He had married a niece of Dietrich Bonhoeffer, the
famous minister who defied Hitler and died in a concentra-
tion camp, and had written Bonhoeffer's official biography.
For three or four years, Bethge came to Lynchburg College
as a visiting professor for one semester each year.

Repeatedly, in lectures at the college and occasional talks
wherever he was invited in the U.S., Bethge warned that he
trembled for our country as he watched the ascending power
of the Falwells and Robertsons and their alliance with political figures like Ronald Reagan. "It is exactly as it began in
Germany in the 1930s," he said. "The government encouraged the Christians who spoke most favorably of its actions
and suppressed the ones who were critical of them." He feared
that a similar thing was occurring in America: certain factions
in church and government were joining forces to take over
the country and abridge its freedoms.

In early 1982, I was invited by a group of clergy and laity
from Jewish, Catholic, and Protestant communities in Madison, Wisconsin, calling themselves Prophetic Alternatives, to

be the keynote speaker for a series of lectures by distinguished theologians titled "Agenda for a Prophetic Faith." I named my contribution "The Fundamentalist Threat to America," and began my speech by enumerating some of the supposed "threats" to America always under indictment by the fundamentalists: communism, socialism, liberalism, secular humanism, pornography, the peace movement, television programming, the National and World Councils of Churches, the decay of the American home, the *Reader's Digest Condensed Version of the Bible,* abortion, fluoridation, the Democratic party, ERA, dancing, homosexuality, and unisex hairstyles.

The fundamentalists, I said, had "campaigned against the rights of women, fought back sex education for young people, exercised indiscriminate censorship in school libraries, won the president's ear on tax exemption for racially-restricted schools, promoted rampant militarism, elected reactionary congressmen, and injected a mood of hatred and divisiveness in this country as damaging as anything we [had] seen since the days of Vietnam and Kent State."

It was time, I proposed, for us to stop "being amused by their antics, their language, and their methods," and to begin "taking them seriously as people who believe and practice the viewpoints they espouse." In other words, it was time "we stopped being polite and considered the threat they themselves represented to the American way of life."

Noting the history of fundamentalism in America and how it had always taken advantage of people's ignorance and prejudices, I commented on how much more adroit and unprincipled today's fundamentalists were in manipulating people's understanding and emotions. They talked endlessly of morality, I said, alluding to the strength of the Moral Majority, but it was not the morality of Jesus. Theirs was "a morality extolling personal success, riches, and worldly happiness, while Jesus represented the willingness to fail and be crucified in the world." Theirs was "a morality devoted to military might, national truculence, and war, while Jesus advocated humility, peace, and turning the other cheek." Theirs was "a morality characterized by legalism, external authority, and punishment, while Jesus died to break the power of these earthly bondages." The truth was, I said, that "the TV evangelists are unprincipled exploiters of popular prejudice, shaping it to their personal service and casting over it a patina of religious devotion."

I discussed the fundamentalists' use of paranoia, and how they exploited people's fears, anxieties, and feelings of persecution. Fundamentalist leaders, I said, played on these subliminal emotions:

Fundamentalist congregations are made to feel rejected, mistreated, and despised by the world, especially by liberals, scientists, industrialists, and anyone else who represents an educational or social elite. "They think we're ignorant," the preachers tell their audiences; "they say we're backward, that we don't understand science and culture and modern biblical criticism, that we're just a bunch of country folks!" There is always a "We'll-show-them" implication in such inflammatory rhetoric. And the human response is to circle the wagons, to draw together against the enemy attack, to hate the faceless and amoral forces out there prepared to burn, pillage, and destroy their way of life.

Falwell, I said, was a natural artist in the use of such tactics. When a professor at Lynchburg College wrote a newspaper column calling attention to contradictions in Falwell's recent utterances about God's not answering Jewish prayers, Falwell attacked the professor on his Sunday broadcast without telling people what the professor had actually said. Not only that, Falwell broadened the scope of the professor's criticism to include his audience as well as himself, something the professor hadn't done.

"We know," said Falwell, "all the chicanery and dishonesty and deception and the absolute hate on the part of some against this ministry and this preacher and against you and what you stand for and the message we preach. That's nothing new. They nailed your Lord to the cross too."

The inflammatory speech continued for approximately six minutes, all as part of the "worship" at Thomas Road Baptist Church.

"The more they bruise and bloody us," Falwell concluded, "the more our people rally together. One thing about our crowd, we don't have any cowards in the bunch. And if you want a fight, you've got one. Our fellows know where the truth is and they know how to tell it and they don't fear anybody. And we thank God for millions of Americans who have made the same commitment. Cal Thomas, will you come and lead us in prayer, please."

Toward the end of my address, I sketched a picture of what American life might look like eighteen years hence, at the end of the twentieth century, if the fundamentalists were not stopped in their search for power and control over the government and all Americans. Their forces would be in charge of the nation, I said. Evolutionary science would be banned from the classroom. There would be government censorship over newspapers, magazines, and television programs. Elections would be limited to born-again Christians, and Jews and blacks would be back where they were in America before World War Two. I said a number of other things too, some of them designed to be outlandish in order to make my audience think.

But now, looking back from twenty-five years later, I think about how much of what I predicted has come true in one form or another. The Monica Goodling investigation revealed that there are approximately 150 graduates of Pat Robertson's Regents University in jobs at the White House, and while there were no figures for the graduates of Liberty University (formerly Liberty Baptist College), Patrick Henry, and other fundamentalist and evangelical schools, their graduates in Washington must number in the thousands. Many fine political candidates have been driven from the field by the religious right's vicious assault on their beliefs, their families, and their character.

I remember sitting in Senator Mark Hatfield's office in the U.S. Senate Building one day while I was a Lynchburg pastor. We were talking about the unprincipled way the religious right funneled lies and innuendoes into political campaigns to defeat their enemies. Hatfield confessed that he had chosen not to run for office again in Oregon. He was one of the finest Christians in Washington, but Jerry Falwell had threatened to smear him if he stood for reelection.

"It's too painful for me and my family," he said. "You spend half your time trying to fight the lies they tell about you, and the other half defending what you've said against the misunderstandings they've managed to generate. At some point, you simply have to decide if it's worth carrying on. Or, at some point, you merely settle for the worst option and say, 'No, it isn't worth it.'"

Falwell's master plan, in those years, called for nothing less than a new, independent denomination consisting of churches he had fostered that would cover the United States like the Baptists or Methodists and do his bidding on a grand scale. Small replicas of Thomas Road Baptist Church, often calling themselves Liberty Baptist Church, emerged everywhere.

Deborah Caldwell, a reporter for the *Dallas Morning News,* recalled in an article titled "Jerry Falwell and Me," which was posted on the Web after Falwell died, how one of these new congregations named Liberty Baptist Church sprang up in her small hometown in Pennsylvania. It had been an idyllic little town, she said, the kind of town everybody in America ought to grow up in—until the advent of the new church. The pastor, trained in Lynchburg, came into the community spoiling for a fight. As his church grew and his voice became more important, it also became more strident, and soon he was pitting one group of people in the town against another. The Norman Rockwellish town became a viper's pit.

Eventually, Falwell would take his own Thomas Road Baptist Church into the Southern Baptist Convention, and it would cease, at least by definition, to be an independent church. But he never stopped mentoring new churches like the one in Caldwell's hometown, and it's a safe bet that the majority of those churches, wherever they are, have a minister cloned in the image of the most pugnacious pastor in America.

FOUR

Life in Falwell's Town

Contrary to what may appear by implication in the previous chapters, I didn't spend a lot of time thinking about Jerry Falwell. I couldn't. I had too many other things on my plate to do that. In addition to writing a weekly sermon and weekly prayers and affirmations for the worship service, which I regarded as the centerpiece of what I was there for, I had a major corporation to run. There were boards and committees to meet, a weekly newsletter to put out, daily hospital calls to make, people to bury, families to console, public affairs to be present for, prospective members to call on, old folks to visit, new members to teach, a staff to direct, and, always, desperately hurting people to counsel. I had never been so busy in my life!

Once, while I was in Lynchburg, a middle-aged man from northern Virginia showed up at the church offices and asked to see me. I didn't have time, but because he had driven so far, I squeezed him in at noon by making a call and delaying a luncheon appointment. He owned a ship-outfitting company, he said. They took orders, designed and manufactured the furnishings, then transported them to the shipyard and installed them. But he had been thinking lately that he might like to become a minister. He belonged to a small Episcopal church in the countryside, and liked sometimes to go there to meditate during the week, when there was never anybody around. His life was too busy, he thought; he needed a profession in which he could be quiet.

I carried the calendar from my desk over to the sofa and sat down beside him. I showed him what my Sunday had been like, and my Monday, and my Tuesday, and my Wednesday, and— By the time I got to Thursday, he was obviously in distress.

"All those meetings," he said. "All those people! How do you have any time for yourself?"

"I don't," I said. "I live in a piranha bowl. So does my wife."

I gave him a copy of *The Tender Shepherd,* a book I had recently published about the pastor's role, and walked him out to his car in the parking lot as I departed for my luncheon engagement. I never heard from him again. He is probably still outfitting ships, because he at least has time occasionally to go down to his little Episcopal church and sit quietly while he meditates.

But I got glimpses of what Jerry Falwell was doing. He was almost always in the news, announcing this program or that one, bragging about the size of his college, condemning secular humanists and homosexuals and abortionists and agnostics and intellectuals, often without taking a breath while moving from one to the other. He didn't attend meetings of the town's ministers, even though he was repeatedly invited. The other ministers all had the impression that he looked down on them. In his eyes, they were pip-squeak pastors who would never amount to a hill of holy beans. His time was too valuable to spend it with them, talking about the city's poor and homeless.

But word about what he was doing was everywhere. Almost everybody I met had a story to tell.

Like one of our church members who was head nurse in the psychiatric department of Baptist Hospital. She had noticed that many of the patients in her ward began the day feeling bright and happy, then, by late afternoon, were often depressed and downbeat. Something—or someone—was affecting their mood, she was convinced.

A small, feisty woman in her early fifties who had raised her children alone and fended off the wolf while doing it, this woman was tough and smart. She knew she could get to the bottom of the problem. So she had a folding screen erected in one of the rooms where there were two patients, and after her morning duties, quietly secreted herself behind it to observe and see if she could figure out what was happening.

She found out the very first day of her stakeout.

Two ministers from Thomas Road Baptist Church came to call on the patients—not just the two patients in that room but all of the patients on the floor. She could hear them making their way, jovially and blusteringly, from room to room. They began by asking the patients if they were saved. Then, whether they said yes or no, they launched into vivid descriptions of what it was going to be like to spend eternity in hell.

But they would intervene for the patients, they said. They were men of God, and had influence with the Almighty. They did it for all the members of Thomas Road Baptist Church, and they did it for people who gave part of their worldly goods to Thomas Road Baptist Church, whether they were members or not.

"Those scoundrels were scaring our patients into donating to their church!" said the nurse. "One of them even said they would bring a lawyer over to change a patient's will!"

She didn't blow her cover that day, even though she was outraged enough to do it. Instead, she went to the hospital board and described what she had witnessed and got the board to forbid the ministers of Thomas Road Baptist Church to visit anybody who wasn't legitimately a member of their congregation.

She still fumes about what they were doing.

Teachers from Liberty Baptist College began coming to our church and quietly asking if they could speak to me.

One of them, a small, elfish-spirited woman named Olga Kronmeyer, who taught poetry and creative writing, said she was there because it was the only job she could get. She hated the regimentation imposed on both the students and the faculty, she said. She hated it that she had to pay a tithe of her income back to Thomas Road Baptist Church. I asked if they had some way of checking on the professors to make sure they did it.

"Oh yes," she chirruped, "they have ways of checking on everything we do!"

She laughed about the hypocrisy of a lot of students. They weren't supposed to hold hands or kiss or have anything to do with members of the opposite sex, she said. They weren't supposed to go to the movies. "They all go down to the theaters in Roanoke," she said, "where they won't run into any of their professors and they can neck and kiss and do anything they want."

She giggled when she told me this.

I guessed that Olga was secretly rebellious. She lived with her aged mother and took care of her. She had to behave herself, she said, because she couldn't afford to lose her job.

Later, when she got braver, she sometimes came to worship at our church. I asked if she wouldn't be missed at Thomas Road. She always said she had been to the early service there so she could come to us at eleven o'clock. Eventually someone in the chain of command at Liberty Baptist College let her know that they were watching her and knew she came across town to First Presbyterian Church. But by that time she had become more self-confident and said they could just fire her if they wanted to.

I imagine she was relatively safe because they considered

her unimportant in the scheme of things. She was, after all, only a woman, and a very slight one at that. As long as she taught her courses and performed the other requisite faculty duties, they would not dismiss her.

Olga was a very clever woman, and often mocked Falwell and Pierre Guillermin, Liberty's president, and other people on campus. She also read me satirical little poems she had written, poking fun at them and at herself for working in a place like Liberty Baptist College. Many of the allusions in her poems were to classical figures and situations, and often I could not follow them by merely listening and not seeing them on paper.

But I always smiled at her and appeared to understand. She was pleased, I think, to have at least one sympathetic friend in the whole town.

Another professor who came to see me several times was a man in his early middle years named Lynn Ridenhour. Lynn had been a Baptist pastor in Missouri and got a master's degree in English from some school so he could hire on as a professor at Liberty Baptist College. It had been a dream of his for some time, he said, and he was very excited about being part of Jerry Falwell's impressive organization. He even became a member of the *Old-Time Gospel Hour* choir.

But Ridenhour's dream had been spoiled soon after his arrival when three different people—two students and one professor—reported him to the dean's office for wearing his light, thinly textured hair combed neatly over his ears. There were very strict codes for everything at Liberty, including how long a person's hair could be. I always thought that was ironic, considering the name of the college.

When Lynn was summoned to the dean's office, he explained that he had a medical reason for the way his hair was coiffed. He had been in a bad car accident. There was a fire, and the tops of both ears were severely burned. The plastic surgeon who reconstructed them told him to wear his hair combed over his ears because direct sunlight might cause cancers on them.

This information produced a quandary for the dean. He dismissed Ridenhour, saying he would consult with the president and Dr. Falwell and they would revisit the matter the next day. When Ridenhour returned, the brilliant solution, apparently reached in consultation with Falwell and Guillermin, was that he should trim his hair neatly according to the college's rules and then wear earmuffs between classes, when he had to go outdoors.

Ridenhour said that was preposterous and that he couldn't stay at Liberty Baptist College if he was to be treated that way. This sent the dean back for another conference with his bosses.

The final upshot of it all was that Ridenhour would be permitted to leave his hair as it was, but must have a letter from his doctor explaining his medical condition, carry the letter with him at all times, and show it to anyone who challenged him about the length of his hair!

Ridenhour clearly thought this was ridiculous, and I think this, more than anything else he encountered on a campus that some people described as being run "like a Nazi boot camp," was the beginning of his complete disillusionment with Falwell and Liberty Baptist College. Often, he came to my office just to let off steam. He had a young wife, and I'm sure he confided in her. But he clearly needed someone in a position of authority to provide a sympathetic ear for his troubles. He said he felt safe with me, and always thanked me for listening to him.

There would be more to his story later—much more—but I shall save that for the time being.

Every year, at Halloween, there was talk around town about the Thomas Road Baptist Church's "Scare Mare," as it was called, an event in which children and young people wandered through a gauntlet of frightening scenes and experiences designed, as one of my elderly church members put it, "to scare the hell out of them."

Many conservative churches made a great show of refusing to allow their members to celebrate what they called "a pagan holiday" glorifying devils and witches. But the students at Thomas Road and Liberty Baptist College apparently had decided to turn the tables by making Halloween into an evangelical occasion.

Each Halloween, according to reports, "Scare Mare" became increasingly imaginative and horrendous, with the result that the children were more and more terrified by encounters with hideous corpses, incredible fiends, and frightening, unearthly scenes, many depicting life in hell.

Then, as the supreme justification for providing this horrific experience, "counselors" were present who talked to them about what it would be like to die without Jesus and go to hell. There were always accounts of dramatic conversions, even of some of the most rascally, rebellious young people who had entered the gamut of scares bragging that they weren't afraid of anything.

Occasionally some of the more adventurous members of my congregation—I remember in particular a young woman, a doctor's daughter, whom I suspected of being a lesbian— told me about having attended Thomas Road Baptist Church "just for the experience of it." They usually experienced a frisson of fear that they would be found out as interlopers and subjected to some form of ridicule, if not outright detention. They could not believe, they said, what a circus it was.

"Circus" was the word they most often associated with it.

There was always a buzz of excitement before the service, they reported. There were many strangers, obviously, people who spoke of being in Lynchburg for the first time, and of traveling from as far away as Baton Rouge or Colorado Springs. This in itself heightened the sense of anticipation in the congregation.

The service was always grandly orchestrated, with a huge choir, lots of lights and TV cameras, pyrotechnics on the organ and piano, special guests, musical personalities, a cadre of ministers, and, typically entering the podium and taking his place after everything else had begun, Falwell himself, the bumptious, smiling center of attention.

The music was important—it was always grand and sweeping in nature, with an emphasis on glorious old gospel favorites, and invariably with soul-touching solos by such dramatic singers as Anita Bryant and Doug Oldham. And distinguished guests imparted a special cachet to the services. Phyllis Schlafly, the famous antifeminist, was a favorite of Falwell's. He often said that she didn't preach, because Baptists didn't have women preachers, but she could talk with the best of them.

It was Falwell himself, the cocky, self-assured owner and manager, the entrepreneur-in-charge, who always provided the real drama of the hour (or hour and a half, actually; it was edited down to an hour for the TV broadcast) when the house lights dimmed and he stepped up to the pulpit as the glowing, puffy-cheeked, magical-voiced don of everything, pastor of Thomas Road Baptist Church, preacher for the *Old-Time Gospel Hour,* founder of the Moral Majority, and the most important religious figure in America!

Howard Fineman, in his *Newsweek* tribute to Falwell after Falwell's death, said of him, "He could be a demagogue, but he was as much a P.T. Barnum as anything else." This was never truer than when he stood in the pulpit of Thomas Road Baptist Church, beaming out over the people who had come from all over the country to see him in person, and began speaking in his confident, emphatic manner about Christ, the Apocalypse, and the times we were living in. He often mentioned Christ in his sermons, but rarely Jesus. This might seem curious in a Baptist preacher, but Falwell always seemed to think in eschatological terms, as if he were seeing a great cosmic battle playing out before his eyes, and didn't have time to review the smaller, more discrete stories about the Jesus of the Gospels that are the plainer fare of lesser preachers.

Dr. James Price, the Lynchburg College professor I have mentioned as an avid Falwell observer, once gave a paper to the Department of Religion at the University of Virginia in which he discussed Falwell's use of the Bible. I do not recall the precise figures he cited, but I remember being surprised at the preponderance of occasions on which Falwell preached from Old Testament texts instead of from the New Testament, where one might reasonably expect a Christian minister to find his greatest inspiration. During a five-year period Price studied, examining all of Falwell's sermons for those years, he said that Falwell spoke from Old Testament texts approximately 85 percent of the time.

This would explain several things about Falwell. First, his comfort with the Old Testament would support his sense of speaking didactically, like the prophets of Israel, and also his certainty that the United States was a nation created by God and therefore under divine judgment. Second, it fit in beautifully with his strongly judgmental character, which saw everything in black and white, without ethical, theological, or philosophical nuances. Third, it allowed him to connect the Bible with the wide panoply of prejudices that formed the background for his Moral Majority program. And, fourth, it rescued him from having to deal with the perennially troubling side of Jesus, who had mercy on sinners and always condemned the posturing of the self-righteous.

There was nothing sophisticated about Falwell. He was a beer-and-chips preacher, a populist who didn't go in for carefully shaded arguments. When he was young, he apparently believed that the Bible was not a literal document at all, but a collection of responsive materials that must be understood over against their times and occasions. At some point, though, he shifted to the rigid fundamentalist position that every word in the entire Bible was ordained by God, possibly because he found that this went down better with his audiences of simple, unsophisticated hearers who wanted to believe that the Bible is impervious like granite to modern criticism and Darwinian science. He didn't thunder "The Bible says" as often as Billy Graham did, but he frequently cited snippets of text, more often than not from the Old Testament—even from an obscure book like Leviticus—as incontrovertible evidence for his judgments and opinions.

From a purely homiletical point of view, there was nothing great about his sermons, or, for that matter, his delivery. He depended more on his authoritative bearing and sonorous voice to sway an audience than on fresh biblical interpretation, cogent argument, or convincing illustrations. I could never decide whether he wrote his sermons or used a ghostwriter; most of the time I gave him the benefit of the doubt, and imagined him sitting at his desk, pen in hand, jotting down a few bold notes as his speaking points, just as he probably had when he began preaching years ago.

I recently asked Jim Price what he thought, and he said

he believed I was right, in the main, but that when Falwell was preaching expository sermons—ones that purported to explain whole passages of Scripture—they were ghostwritten and he merely read them. This no doubt accounted for his appearing somewhat bored by them, and for the fact that occasionally, while reading one of them, he would pause, say, "Isn't it amazing!" and go off on a tangent that was much more interesting than the sermon itself.

The real secret of Jerry Falwell's command when he stood to preach lay in his bearing itself—erect, confident, with clipped words and strong projection. He was, after all, Jerry Falwell, the CEO of a small empire, the man who liked to take charge wherever he was. He preached every Sunday to men and women who knew more about the Bible and had a better grasp of theology than he did, and probably to some who could speak more engagingly. But he was the Big Dog, and everything about him said that he was, so others listened to him.

A couple of times, while I was in Lynchburg, I received telephone calls from Baptist ministers asking if they could hold luncheon meetings at our church to talk about things they didn't want their secretaries and other ministers to overhear. Because they knew I was outspoken about Falwell, they considered our church a sanctuary where they could come and be themselves. What they really needed to discuss, both times, was how to survive amid all the false expectations Falwell's success generated in their congregations.

There were six or seven men in this group. All were well educated, with liberal arts and seminary degrees—the latter usually from one of the Southern Baptist seminaries—and all were mature, thoughtful ministers. The problem, they explained, was the model of ministry Falwell had forced on them because they operated in the same community as he. Their churches all wanted big, flamboyant choirs like his, and fleets of buses and radio and TV shows. And they expected their pastors to be as forthright and declarative as Falwell in confronting the sins of the day, denouncing communism and homosexuality and abortion and integration and secular humanism.

One pastor, the Reverend Nathan Brooks of Peakland Baptist Church, led a small, moderate congregation on a lovely, tree-lined street very close to our church. Nathan was a tall, comfortable-looking man in his late forties who had had extensive training in pastoral care and was a wonderful, warmhearted minister to his flock, nurturing them in biblical faith and gently tending them in times of joy and sorrow. He was, in many ways, the very antithesis of Jerry Falwell.

Yet Nathan suffered from the contrast. There were people in his church who complained that he was not dynamic enough, that their church's membership was not swelling under his leadership, that he was lovable but not dramatic and forceful enough to compel people's attention. I can't count the number of times I heard that Nathan was on the ropes, about to lose his congregation, and he would always patiently weather the storm and be there when it was over.

He reminded me of a story I read once in *The Atlantic* about a little burro on a Western ranch that was used to break unruly steers. The cowboys yoked it to the steer they wanted to tame and turned the two loose into the desert. Off they would go, with the steer horribly mistreating the burro, sometimes even jerking on the yoke to fling the burro over its back, and be gone for days. But eventually the two would come back to the ranch, the little burro trotting along home and the steer following meekly in its wake. Peakland Baptist Church sometimes had rebel members who wanted to get rid of Nathan, but he always wore them down, and stayed as their minister until he was ready to retire.

I saw him a couple of years ago when I was speaking at Lynchburg College and the First Christian Church in Lynchburg. He and his wife had joined the Christian Church (Disciples of Christ) and he had an office there from which to practice pastoral care. He was as radiantly sweet and joyous as ever!

Another of the Baptist ministers was a bright, feisty young man named Don Norman. Don had a thriving church, the Randolph Memorial Baptist Church in Madison Heights, a couple of miles north of Lynchburg, and had the same name as one of Falwell's lieutenants at that time. He said he sometimes got telephone calls in the middle of the night from people who thought he was the other Don Norman. Once, the caller had rattled on about some secret plans or other that Don said he knew he wasn't supposed to be hearing. It took the caller two or three minutes to realize he didn't have Falwell's associate. Then he demanded to know who it was he was talking to. Don said, "I think you have the wrong Don Norman," and hung up.

I felt sorry for these ministers. They didn't deserve the

extra grief they were getting for having their churches so close to Falwell's. Being a Baptist minister is hard enough at any time, in any place. But being one in Lynchburg in the 1980s was cruel and unusual punishment, and I wouldn't have wished it on my worst enemy.

Falwell might have done more for the other ministers if he had been more brotherly. But he was always an independent man, going his own way. At that time, he had not yet joined the Southern Baptist Convention, though he was often invited to speak at their pastors' conference when the convention met. He joined a few years later, as I understand it, because he wanted to get the thousand dollars the Southern Baptist Convention was awarding to its colleges, universities, and seminaries for each of the students enrolled in their institutions.

Falwell was funny that way. He liked to be independent, but he could also make concessions when he had to in order to get what he needed. He wanted to get his college accredited by the Southern Association of Schools and Colleges because accreditation was necessary to having his student teachers approved for training, to having his sports teams play in regular intercollegiate associations, and to meeting any other professional standards required by various accrediting agencies. At first he spoke derisively of the SASC and other accrediting agencies, contending that God's was the only accreditation Liberty Baptist College needed. But as pressure mounted for his school to become duly accredited, he gave in and began submitting to the process of meeting standards.

One standard had to do with the library. Falwell himself

was not a scholar and didn't value having a research library on Liberty Baptist College's campus. He always distrusted professors who were too scholarly. But when the SASC levied black marks against Liberty's library, Falwell behaved characteristically: he went up North, bought some old libraries, and had their books moved to Lynchburg. At the same time, he ordered statements pasted in the front of many of these books saying they were inappropriate for Liberty Baptist College students to read. He capitulated to the SASC's regulations about having the books, but he wouldn't permit his students to use them!

Falwell could also be charming when he wanted to be. Professor Harvey Cox, the popular religion teacher at Harvard University, was dying to meet him and see him in action, so he wangled an invitation for Falwell to address the students at Harvard Business School. Cox took a lot of flack from students and fellow professors, but Falwell performed graciously and won kudos from many who heard him on that occasion.

The same thing happened when Bishop William H. Willimon, then minister to Duke University, invited him to speak in Duke Chapel. Writing about the occasion in *The Christian Century,* Willimon said having Falwell at Duke nearly cost him his job because of the enormous number of protests he and Duke's president received. Yet Falwell handled the students tactfully and appealingly, and, when attacked by one student for having so few blacks at Liberty Baptist College, did a mea culpa, apologizing that Liberty's student body was only 12 percent African American, then

asked what the ratio of blacks to whites was at Duke. There
was a silence, as none of the students or faculty present
seemed to know.

But Falwell knew. "I'll tell you," he said. "Six percent. Six
percent! Your endowment is fifty times bigger than ours. You
have had years to work on this issue (though admittedly you
spent half of your life as a racially segregated school). In fact,
I struggled with whether the Lord wanted me to come here
tonight to a school that, though you have been given great
gifts, has such a poor record of minority enrollment. I pray
that you will let the Lord help you do better in this area."

This is the Falwell we can only wish we had seen more of.

With his flair for entrepreneurialism, Falwell constantly
bragged about how many students were now signed up for
degree programs at Liberty Baptist College. As some of his
professors said, they would like to see all of the students he
said they had. Having been a college administrator myself, I
knew how easily enrollment figures could be manipulated
and inflated. Falwell simply had to count all the part-time
students and visitors to special campus events and use those
numbers to swell his statistical reports. He understood the
old business principle that "success begets success."

The enrollment was doubtless growing, though, because
Falwell was constantly urging *The Old-Time Gospel Hour* audience to send money to build new dormitories and
classrooms, and these buildings were hastily going up on the
little foothills below Liberty Mountain. On one occasion,

Falwell sent out an urgent letter to his subscribers saying that they had had to halt all construction until the subscribers sent more money. A reporter who went out to check on the truth of this said that the Caterpillars, cement machines, and hammers were all still going at full tilt!

One morning I had a telephone call from Will Campbell, the noted antisegregationist and author of *The Convention, Forty Acres and a Goat,* and other best-selling books. He had been speaking at Hampton-Sidney College the night before and someone from the college had driven him to the airport and dropped him off a little before plane time. But a thick fog had prevented the landing of the commuter plane that usually stopped in Lynchburg in the morning and there would not be another until two o'clock. Will wanted to know if I could possibly come and get him for a few hours' visit.

My schedule was as cluttered as usual, but I said I would be at the airport in twenty minutes. Will was wearing a brand-new broad-brimmed black Stetson when I got to the terminal. "Ah, Will," I said, "you have to keep up your image now, don't you?" I don't know how widely known it is, but he was the real-life model for the Reverend Will B. Dunn, the hapless, stogie-smoking cleric of Doug Marlette's popular cartoon strip *Kudzu,* who always wore a wide-brimmed black hat.

"What would you like to do?" I asked. "We've got at least a couple of hours before lunch."

"Well," drawled Will, pulling at his chin as he often did, "I'd like to see your church. And I wouldn't mind seeing this Baptist college where Falwell hangs out."

We were not far from Liberty Baptist College, so I made that our first stop. It was just off the bypass. I paused at the guard's station and explained that I was escorting a visiting clergyman from Nashville who wanted to see the college. I didn't tell him who I was, and hoped he wouldn't ask. He didn't. He gave us a little card to put inside the windshield, told us to have a nice day, and motioned us through.

Almost all the dorms at Liberty Baptist College, in those days at least, were built the same way—same size, same red bricks, same undistinguished rectangular architecture. Some sat on hilltops, others on the side of the hill, and others in the vale. The college looked more like a large, orderly prison than an educational institution.

"Hell," said Will Campbell, staring around in disbelief. "This ain't nuthin' but a bunch o' redbrick chicken coops!"

He was right. And the classroom buildings weren't much different. They had all been erected as swiftly and inexpensively as possible. I could imagine how disappointed a lot of students must have been when they signed up by mail to come to Liberty Baptist College and then got there and viewed such a surrealistically plain, undecorated campus. But the buildings were functional, and I'm sure it was Falwell's decision to make them that way. He wasn't one for frittering money and embellishments on anything, not even the sanctuary of Thomas Road Baptist Church. His aim was to get the students there, give them what passed for an education at Liberty Baptist College, and pour them out into churches and schools all over Virginia and eventually all over the United States, where they would change the course of

American life and politics. A bunch of redbrick chicken coops was sufficient for that!

The one thing Jerry owned that spelled class was a Lear jet. Howard Fineman said Falwell told him, one day in 1980 when Fineman was boarding the plane with him, that it had been "specially reconfigured by an Israeli company." The way I heard it was that the Israelis had given the plane to Falwell, and I never had any reason to believe otherwise.

In his role as a founder of Christian Zionism, Falwell made a number of trips to Israel, and Israeli leaders who came to Washington frequently came to Lynchburg as well. Menachem Begin said he never came to the United States without seeing his friend Falwell.

During my years at Vanderbilt University, my cubbyhole in the faculty mail room was often full of thick propaganda envelopes from B'nai B'rith, promoting the nation of Israel and pleading the cause of Jews around the world. My mailbox wasn't the only one; they were all that way. I used to think that the Jews could make better use of their money. Then, one day, the barrage of propaganda stopped. Somebody at B'nai B'rith had got wise. They spent their money on an airplane for the leader of the Moral Majority, who could—and did—do more for the cause of Israel than anyone else in America. Within five years of the day Falwell took possession of his Lear jet, every evangelist and conservative religious figure in this country was pro-Israel.

Falwell told me once that he never liked to be away from home overnight, and having his own plane helped him to avoid that most of the time. He jetted to meetings all over the country, and could speak at rallies in Cleveland, Chicago, and St. Louis all in the same day and then be home for dinner with his wife, Macel. Sometimes he even flew to California, spoke at a rally, and was back home before nightfall.

But that wasn't the most important use of the jet. Not to a hustler like Jerry Falwell.

Once, twice, sometimes three times a week, Falwell's jet plane was dispatched to National Airport in Washington, D.C., to pick up a member of Congress, a Cabinet member, or some other important figure in American politics, and bring him to Lynchburg to speak at the 9:20 A.M. chapel service at Liberty Baptist College. When chapel was over, Falwell handed the speaker an envelope containing a handsome honorarium—I was told that the standard figure was $10,000, paid out of *Old-Time Gospel Hour* funds—and then he was whisked back to the capital in time for lunch.

It wasn't any wonder that Falwell claimed—I heard him say it more than once—that he could walk into the Oval Office on five minutes' notice any day he chose. He was on first-name speaking terms with practically every member of Congress and most of the president's cabinet. Some of them liked and admired him, and some hated him. But the important thing to Falwell was that he knew them and they knew him.

That was part of what put the swagger in his gait.

It was his role in bringing faith and politics together that Falwell will be remembered for in all the history books. Not for his preaching, which was bold but not memorable. Not for his pastoral leadership, which was never an end in itself.

But for his wheeling and dealing in the world of politics, where he fancied himself a deal broker and a king maker. That is where he was at his best, and, whether we approve of his character or not, where we have to admire his talent. He was Karl Rove before there was a Karl Rove.

Recently, in Lynchburg, I said to Dr. Wilbur Burger, a local oncologist who knew Falwell and had treated members of his family, that if Falwell hadn't been a preacher he would have been a politician.

"He *was* a politician," said Wilbur.

Then, after a moment's thought, he added, "A *consummate* politician."

You can't always trust salesmen who are as eager for a sale as Falwell was. They cut corners, shade the truth, ignore the rules, and dive for the finish line. It is their nature, and it was Falwell's nature. He appears not to have been troubled by ethics, the way some people are. For him, the ends always justified the means. Always.

I remember one of his shenanigans that at the time I thought was so reprehensible that afterward I could never really trust him. It was in 1979 and 1980, after the end of the Vietnam War and the displacement of millions of people from South Vietnam. Many of them crowded into boats and put out to sea, hoping for clemency from some country—any country—that would take them in and give them a place to live. There were frequently sad stories in the papers about whole boatloads of people who were lost in a storm or assaulted by pirates who robbed them of their valuables, raped their women, and left them destitute.

Someone at the *Old-Time Gospel Hour*—it may have been Falwell himself—realized what a touching drama these poor, lost souls offered to the sentimental people of the world and figured out a way to profit from their distress. Falwell began announcing that *OTGH* was sponsoring a massive effort to relocate Vietnamese boat people on property they would purchase in South America, and invited their viewers to send tax-deductible donations to *OTGH* for this purpose.

The land in South America was jungle land. I don't know if any reporter ever checked to be certain a single piece of property was bought and paid for by *OTGH,* or if any immigrants were ever settled there. The point, never actually stated, but naturally implied, was that no Americans were going to be displaced or troubled by the sudden appearance of all those foreigners on our shores. They would be settled on jungle soil in South America—presumably land akin to what they had been forced to abandon in Vietnam.

The real kicker in this story, though, lies in a brief message that appeared briefly in small print—very small print— each time *OTGH*'s ad was flashed on the TV screen. What it said was that anything collected "in excess of $100,000" would be used by the *Old-Time Gospel Hour.* It didn't say what for. It probably wasn't meant to be noticed at all. It was simply there to give *OTGH* an excuse for scarfing down the enormous amount of money raised by this ploy— more than $5 million in the first year alone!

OTGH pulled a similar stunt, but on a slightly smaller

scale, in the early 1980s when it grandly announced a program of feeding the homeless. They acquired a warehouse building a couple of miles from downtown Lynchburg, outfitted it as a kind of supermarket, filled the shelves with food products, had then vice president George H.W. Bush down to cut the ribbon, and filmed the first homeless persons being let loose in the place with shopping carts they would load with free provisions. Touched by the plight of the homeless, who were big in the news at the time, and by *OTGH*'s magnanimous gesture, people all over America sent donations to help pay for this generous arrangement.

What people outside Lynchburg didn't know, and even many inside the town didn't hear, was that the citizens receiving free food at *OTGH*'s food bank were actually members of Thomas Road Baptist Church, and no one else was permitted to enter the premises. Besides, as social workers in Lynchburg said to one another, why would anybody put a food bank for poor families miles away from any place they were likely to live? *OTGH* certainly didn't provide free transportation to the store for them.

I don't know exactly how long the free food deal lasted. I heard different stories. Some said it was closed down almost immediately, after George H. W. Bush had been photographed with Falwell and went back to Washington. Others said it was rarely open, and then only for a couple of hours a day, when the select few were permitted to collect a few groceries, and that it merely disappeared from existence within weeks of its opening.

The point is, it was a sham, like so many things Falwell

and his associates staged in order to get money from faithful viewers. They did get money, that's for sure. Widows and widowers and elderly couples all over America sent in their tithes and offerings to support the work of "that nice man Jerry Falwell." He was doing God's work, and they wanted to have a part in it.

Once, when my wife, Anne, and I were visiting her father, a widower in his mideighties in a small town in Kentucky, he showed us a letter he had received from the *Old-Time Gospel Hour* thanking him for a donation. I don't remember how much it was—maybe a hundred dollars—but he was very proud of having done it. "I watch him every day on TV," the old man said. He lived alone and the television was company to him. He thought Jerry Falwell was speaking directly to him when he asked for money, and he was proud to have sent something.

We didn't say anything. We didn't want to spoil his pleasure.

Later, we learned that Anne's brother, who was a vice president of Sears in Chicago, had contributed to *OTGH* and asked that one of Falwell's special Bibles be sent to his father in Kentucky. The Bible was sent, and their father's name was added to the computer list for solicitation.

All very clever!

I don't mean to imply that Jerry Falwell was a crook. I think he was simply a man on a mission who would hesitate at nothing to accomplish the mission. He could inveigh against welfare on Sunday and on Monday watch the new students at Liberty being trundled down to the local welfare offices to sign up for food stamps and medical service. He wasn't being duplicitous. He merely had his eye on the goal, which was to build a mighty Christian empire—"Christian" as he understood Christian—centered in his hometown of Lynchburg, whatever it cost to build it.

Probably only people who have received some sense of divine calling can fully understand what made a man like Falwell behave as he did. From the time he was a young man going into the ministry, Falwell believed that God had some special purpose for his existence, and he was committed to fulfilling that purpose whatever the cost. I'm very different from Falwell—almost at the other end of the spectrum, in most ways—but I understand what made him tick. If I hadn't been fortunate enough to get an education and live with one foot in the academic world, I might well have ended up the same way. But I doubt if I would have been as successful as Falwell. He had a true gift for getting what he wanted.

FIVE

The Slippery Slope

While I was busy in my pastoral work and absorbing all this knowledge about Falwell and his projects, I was also flying around the country to speak at various universities, seminaries, and churches. Normally I lectured on preaching, personal spirituality, or pastoral work, depending on what those who invited me asked me to do.

I gave a series of lectures at Princeton Theological Seminary's Summer Institute that was later published as *Christ and the Seasons of Ministry*. There was a lot of interest, at that time, in the seasons of life. Gail Sheehy had written an immensely popular book called *Passages: The Predictable Crises in*

Adult Life. Daniel Levenson had published *The Seasons of a Man's Life.* Now in midlife myself, I was very conscious of how different we all are in the various segments of our lives, and applied the idea to the minister's journey.

But in most places I visited, whatever the formal assignment I was meant to fulfill, I was always asked about what it was like to live in Lynchburg, Virginia, with Jerry Falwell. Everybody knew Falwell. He was in the news almost daily. Most ministers admired him but also despised him, or at least despised his tactics and many of the astounding pronunciamentos he uttered. To them, I was the "expert" on Falwell. They hung on my reflections as if they were gospel.

They were particularly interested in any "reprisals" I suffered for speaking out about Falwell. I was always careful not to accuse Falwell himself of anything, because I honestly did not know the source of any harassment my family and I received. But there were at least reprisals in general, and I did not hesitate to mention them.

In addition to the death threats, phone taps, and early trash pickups I have mentioned, plus the frequent letters to the editor in the local paper that accused me of everything from sheer orneriness to demon possession, there were two other interesting developments.

One day, out of the blue, I had a phone call in which the caller began making strange inquiries about my mailing address, some people I heard from by mail, and whether I had noticed that any of my mail had been missing. When I stopped answering questions until I knew more about the caller's identity, he gave me his name and some official information indicating that he was a federal investigator for the U.S. Postal Service. A pile of mail addressed to me, he said, had been discovered burning on Liberty Mountain— the land where Thomas Road Baptist Church, Liberty Baptist College, and the Moral Majority offices were located. The evidence, according to this man, pointed to an employee in one of the local postal stations who had been funneling some of my mail to one of the Falwell organizations. He did not say which one.

This news clarified a mystery for us. Many times, we had friends or church members calling us to say that we hadn't answered an invitation to a dinner party, a reception, or a rehearsal dinner for a wedding. My wife's response was usually, "We didn't receive your invitation." It happened so frequently that we were beginning to suspect that the U.S. Postal Service wasn't doing a very good job of delivering our mail.

But it wasn't just at home. Occasionally I received a letter at the church that had been stamped "Not at the *Old-Time Gospel Hour.*" This was very puzzling, and the news that our mail was being intentionally delivered to the *OTGH* station suddenly explained everything.

Two or three times in the next few weeks, I heard from this investigator again, saying that he was getting close to wrapping up his case and that I would be hearing from his department. Then I ceased to hear from him. I telephoned the district postal manager and asked for the man who had been working on my case. I was stonewalled. I called a different office. This time I was told that the man had been reassigned. I asked for a forwarding number. I was told that he was unavailable.

The whole thing remains a mystery to me. Was that man really an employee of the U.S. Postal Service or was the whole business only a ruse? If he was who he said he was, why was there no follow-up by the postal service? Was he called or warned off the case? If he wasn't who he said he was, what was the purpose of the calls and the caller's pretending to be something he wasn't?

The second interesting development involved another government agency, the Internal Revenue Service.

Four ministers in Lynchburg were simultaneously targeted by the IRS for extensive audits of our federal tax returns. Two were James J. H. Price, my part-time associate and professor of religion at Lynchburg College, and his colleague William Goodman, who were coauthors of the collection of Falwell's self-contradictory statements. Another was the Reverend George Bean, rector of St. John's Episcopal Church, who had taught a Sunday school class in which there were some frank discussions of the Moral Majority and its emphases. The fourth was yours truly.

Each of us was subjected to a slow, agonizing review by an IRS agent who went over our reports with a fine-tooth comb, not for one year but for three years in a row. Each year, we would no more than wipe our brows and breathe a sigh of relief when here would come the notice of yet another audit!

Poor Jim Price, I think, got the nastiest auditor and received the pickiest treatment. He had claimed some mileage for business travel to a few places where he had spoken, but could not substantiate his actual expenditures. He had reported the amount he had received in honoraria, which should have been proof enough of his having spent the modest amount of money to get there that he was claiming. But the agent insisted on more solid data, and Jim ended up having to pay not only additional taxes but interest and a penalty on the taxes, which, on his college professor's salary, was a genuine hardship.

My auditor appeared to be somewhat embarrassed at utilizing my time on such a fool's errand, and ended up assessing me a few dollars on some small matter that did not amount to much. I forget what it was, but it was negligible. In the end, the experience actually saved me money, because the auditor showed me some deductions I could have been taking but wasn't, and I employed them in the future.

I was lecturing to a group of ministers at a church in Murfreesboro, Tennessee, when someone asked about reprisals from the Falwell camp. I remember commenting that I thought it more than a little odd that the only four men in Lynchburg who had publicly offended Falwell in some way were all being investigated by the IRS and that it had been going on with each of us for three years.

I thought the man who seemed so interested in our tax problems was only a minister who was incensed by what I had said. Later, after I returned home, I learned two things. One was that the man was actually a reporter, not a minister. And the other was that there had been a Falwell spy in our midst who apparently lost no time phoning his superior in Lynchburg to say that I had accused Falwell of pulling strings with the IRS to harass Jim, Bill, George, and me.

Miraculously, the investigations stopped. No more questions. No more meetings. No more audits. Period.

Now, was that merely a coincidence, or did someone at the Falwell headquarters call off the dogs? Why would the four of us have been investigated for three years running? That was not customary procedure, according to all the information I was able to gather. Normally, if an audit did not result in significant discoveries of fraud and/or recovery of money for the IRS, the IRS did not audit the same taxpayer a second year. Certainly not a third year.

Later, when I learned the kind of access Falwell had to government circles, and how easy it was for him to command favors from those circles, I believed the worst about both of these interesting experiences: that there had indeed been an official investigator from the U.S. Postal Service looking into the discovery of some of my mail on Liberty Mountain, and that there had also been hanky-panky involved in the triple-year audits of the IRS reports of four persons who had been openly critical of Falwell.

Somehow, in all of this, I began to realize that I was in a war. I never liked to think negatively. My wife, in fact, always accused me of being too blithely optimistic about everything. I was, she reminded me, like the young man who received a bucket of horse manure for his birthday and immediately set out to look for the horse that must have been his real present. But now I sensed that there were evil forces in the world—the kind of forces of which Saint Paul spoke in the New Testament—invisible, invidious powers that often seek our destruction when we are least aware of it.

It was ironic. Falwell was always talking about the conservatives' war with the liberals, the ACLU, the communists, the ERA, pornographers, homosexuals, abortionists, and everybody else he disagreed with. Now I was sensing that he was right, we *were* in a war. The shelling was going on all the time. Life itself had become a battlefield.

I began to notice a recurrent pattern of resistance in my preaching—notes and asides in sermons, sometimes whole sermons, in which I felt that I had to take on the Moral Majority and fundamentalism in general.

In a sermon called "The Packaging of the Gospel," I protested against the kind of promotionalism that was skewing former understandings of what religion is all about, the slick, glossy packaging that was distorting the true nature of belief.

That is often what happens when the gospel gets mixed up with packaging. For example, consider what it becomes under most TV evangelism, with its red-white-and-blue-spangled sets, its sexily scrubbed young men and women singing religiously erotic music, its endless parade of religious celebrities, its 800 numbers for phoning in donations, and its nattily tailored star evangelists with their dental caps and artfully styled coiffures. These men are the Johnny Carsons of Galilee, the Don Ameches of 24-hour broadcasting. They have completely lost the simple note of authenticity that was heard in Jesus of Nazareth, who owned no super-chariots, had no wardrobe, and would have objected vociferously to such gimmicks as Jerusalem T-shirts and "Yahweh First" pins.

I said I knew that some of my listeners would be uneasy at this kind of attack on their favorite media personalities, but that I really wanted them to understand how dangerous this kind of distortion of the Gospel really is.

Suppose the gospel *à la* TV evangelists were the only gospel to be heard for the next fifty years. What would the church of fifty years from now look like? There would be no congregations of saints as we now know them. People would sit in their own homes before the TV set, munching Fritos and listening to ever greater pleas to "Save this ministry." They would never sing the great songs of the faith, never bow to pray, never reach out to take another human hand. Christianity would become something out of *Brave New World,* to be tuned in between ball games and soap operas. The whole emphasis on following Jesus and preparing for true sacrifice would be lost, or replaced by the repugnant doctrine of the TV preachers that God will send extraordinary blessings on those who support their programs.

I told the story of two young women who had come to my office because they believed "a local evangelist's" promise—patently Falwell's—that if they would "step out on belief" God would give them what they asked. They were so excited about this leap of faith that they sold their house in Connecticut and moved to Lynchburg to be near the preacher who had convinced them they would be cared for. A year later, they were tired of the TV lights in the preacher's church and tired of waiting for their success to arrive. They had spent all the money from the sale of their house, they were broke, and they hadn't been able to find suitable jobs.

"We have been trying the Lord," they said to me in a pleading voice, "and he has not come through. What must we do now?"

"TV Christianity," I said, "is producing a generation of believers whose view of life is so distorted that they do not know how to cope with the simple realities of human existence. They have almost no grasp of the great suffering necessary to overcome the injustices in society. Their Jesus is a plastic Jesus with no real wounds, no crown of thorns, no horrible cross on his back. He is an antiseptic little Jesus huckstered like cars and laxatives and deodorant soaps, without enough real gospel, as a British preacher once put it, to save a titmouse."

In a sermon titled "When Religion Makes You Sick," I outlined some simple tests for telling when one's religion is wholesome and good:

1. Does my religion give me a greater sense of free-dom and self-acceptance than I had before?
2. Does my religion fill me with a sense of love and relationship to the world and to other persons around me?
3. Does my religion make me more tolerant of the beliefs and backgrounds and lifestyles of others?
4. Does my religion impel me to share my life and property with those who have less than I, and gen-erally to become more involved in making a better world for everybody?

I didn't say anything about the new evangelical and fun-damentalist religion, but, given my stance on such religion, I'm sure everybody knew that the sermon was at one level an indictment of it.

For Reformation Day in 1983, I preached on the subject "Toppling Sacred Altars." The text was Judges 6:25–32, about God's sending Gideon, a farmboy, to destroy the altar of Baal, the pagan fertility God, and erect in its place an altar to the living God. This was what the Reformers were sent to do, I said, and it is what those of us who stood in the tra-dition of Luther and Calvin and Zwingli and Knox were meant to do as well.

I didn't directly refer to the televangelists and their sacred altars, but there could have been no mistaking the allusion in this paragraph of the sermon: "Philip Watson, the theolo-gian, wrote a book about Luther a few years ago. He called it *Let God Be God,* for that, he said, was the central message of everything Luther said and did. Let God be God. Stop worshiping a system that pretends to be God. Stop propping up human authorities who love to parade in grandeur and make pronouncements as if they were God. Let *God* be God."

Reading these sermons today, I can see the strain I was under, the way I was putting my shoulder to the wheel and trying to move my people forward, away from the crass materialism and blatant authoritarianism of the most popular religion of the day and on to a reaffirmation of the faith of Jesus and Augustine and Luther and Wesley, which rebelled against every attempt at coercion and restriction, insisting that God didn't make human beings to fit into a cookie-cutter religion.

And I can see why Falwell began to fear what was being preached in the Presbyterian pulpit across town.

Oh, I am not under any illusions about how much I hurt or didn't hurt Falwell. I was a mere slip of a David with only a few stones in my pouch to aim at the presiding Goliath in Lynchburg, and there was no way my sermons or my pronouncements were going to mortally wound him. Annoy him, maybe. They were only gnat bites, in the end. But even gnat bites can become unpleasant if the gnats are persistent.

It was during this indeterminate warfare that one of my members stepped in to try to make peace between Falwell and me. Maybe "make peace" is to put too grand a design on what he did. At least he wanted to get us together.

Les Stone was an upbeat, happy-talking man with the neatest hair in town. It was snow white and lay like a finely combed mop on his head, drawn slightly forward to provide a fetching shock of it across his forehead. The forehead itself was nicely tanned, as Les was retired and played a lot of golf. The total effect was awesome. Everybody said so.

Les was basically very conservative, but he also loved First Presbyterian Church and, because I was its pastor, loved me as well. He had loved Jerry Falwell even longer, and it distressed him that I didn't seem to like or agree with Jerry. Once, he even came into my secretary's office and sat and wept because I seemed to be opposed to his longtime idol. So one day, in the midst of our warfare, Les invited Jerry and me to have lunch at his house.

Les's wife, Florence, a snappy little woman who always seemed truer to me than Les, prepared our meal and served it, but then she excused herself and vanished, leaving the three of us alone in the dining room to eat and discuss things.

At first it was, as the reader can well imagine, a little awkward. We said polite things about the room, the table, the food. We may even have said something nice about one another. Les was sitting at the end of the table and Jerry and I were sitting across from one another.

"Jerry," I said, hoping to break the ice and talk about things that mattered, "those of us on my end of the theological spectrum accept you and your friends as Christians. Why don't you reciprocate and think of us as Christians too?"

He was apparently embarrassed at such a direct question. He murmured something about "the slippery slope."

"What?" I asked. It was the first time I had ever heard the expression.

"The slippery slope," he repeated. "You know, if you start down that way you may not be able to go back."

I wasn't sure what that had to do with my question, unless he meant that if the fundamentalists got to liking the moderates and liberals too much they wouldn't be able to recover their real stance.

Soon, in the halting conversation, I asked him a question about biblical inerrancy. I said I read the Bible and always preached from it, but in my experience there were a lot of discrepancies and inaccuracies in the Scriptures. For example, I pointed out, the synoptic Gospels—Matthew, Mark, and Luke—all set Jesus' cleansing of the temple in Jerusalem at the end of his ministry, as part of the prelude to his crucifixion, while the Gospel of John sets it at the very beginning of Jesus' ministry. Why was that? Did God make a mistake, or forget that he had said it one way in the synoptics and then said it another way in John?

I wasn't trying to be facetious. I was merely trying to underline the importance of the discrepancy.

Jerry's reply: "When I was a student at Baptist Bible College in Missouri, I had a professor who explained that all very well to my satisfaction."

Period.

That was it.

He didn't elaborate. I didn't want to ask him to tell me the explanation, in case he had forgotten it. That would be embarrassing.

The whole conversation went that way. I was lobbing questions and Jerry was either bunting or refusing to take them at all. He didn't ask me anything. Les didn't participate at all. He left it to us to carry on.

I went back to my church disappointed. I hadn't wanted to bait Falwell, but I did want us to have a discussion that would help us to understand one another better. What I understood was that he was shy about discussing important matters with someone he probably regarded as a scholar. It wasn't any wonder that he denigrated "intellectuals." He felt insecure around them.

I have mentioned Professor Lynn Ridenhour, who taught English at Liberty Baptist College. It was about the time of my first meeting with Falwell that he came to me with the news that he had been fired and was out of a job. He was very upset, as his wife was seven and a half months pregnant and they didn't have any money to relocate. It was also in the middle of a semester, which made it impossible for him to find work as a teacher in another institution.

The firing came because Ridenhour and his wife were conducting a Bible study in their home, and, as they were charismatics, had begun attaching faith-healing sessions to it. Falwell was ambivalent about charismatics. On one hand, he feared them and insisted that the age of miracles had ended with the time of the Apostles. This was, he said, "the Baptist position." On the other hand, charismatics were very strong at the time and growing in influence. Many of his donors were charismatics, or at least watched Oral Roberts, Jimmy

Swaggart, Bob Tilton, and Jim and Tammy Bakker, all openly charismatic.

Later, when Jim Bakker went to prison for issuing fraudulent leases on the retirement city he was building, Falwell would go to the Bakkers with open arms and promise to be the caretaker of the *PTL Club* ministry until they could resolve their problems. As it turned out—Tammy Bakker has said this many times—Falwell was a wolf in sheep's clothing who only wanted to get his hands on the Bakkers' satellite, something he had never been able to buy for his own *Old-Time Gospel Hour.* He became the MC for their charismatic program until there was a rebellion in his own ranks from people who remembered his opposition to charismatics and stopped giving to the *Old-Time Gospel Hour.*

When word of the Ridenhours' charismatic meetings reached the executive offices of Liberty Baptist College, Lynn was dismissed without further hearing. Falwell apparently thought he was trying to undermine the college and *OTGH,* where he sang in the choir, by knowingly flouting Falwell's teachings. Ridenhour said his wife became hysterical when he told her he had been fired, because she was afraid they would not have enough money to live on. He returned to Falwell and begged for a little more time. Falwell relented and said he could stay until the end of the semester.

At this point, the Ridenhour story becomes a little confusing, because Lynn himself has told more than one version of it. Sitting in my office at the First Presbyterian Church, he told me he had agreed to write an article for *Penthouse* magazine about what it was like to be a professor at Jerry Falwell's college. He said he decided to do it in order to make a lot of money in a hurry. It was top secret, he said; nobody at the college must know he was doing it. But he had told a colleague whom he trusted, and the colleague went straight to President Guillermin and ratted him out.

One afternoon, three of Falwell's security guards—Ridenhour called them "goons"—appeared at his office and demanded a copy of the article he was writing, plus any notes he had made for it. He told them he wasn't writing an article, when, in fact, he told me he had it at home, not at his office in the college. Searching his office and finding nothing, the guards appeared undecided about what to do. One guard commented that nobody bucked Falwell and lived to tell about it. Then, Ridenhour told me, one of them telephoned a friend who worked for the FBI and asked what they should do. The FBI agent told him to confiscate Ridenhour's typewriter ribbon and they could put it in the lab and reconstruct whatever he had written. They did take the ribbon, and finally released Ridenhour. He had been detained for two or three hours.

That evening, Ridenhour said, he attended the Wednesday-night service at Thomas Road Baptist Church and heard Falwell announce that they had a Judas in their midst who needed to come forward during the hymn of invitation, confess his sin, and be forgiven. Ridenhour remained where he was, but knew his time at the college was definitely over.

He began consulting local attorneys, trying to find someone to represent him in a suit against the college for unlawful detention and defamation of character. No one in Lynchburg would go up against Jerry Falwell in such an inflammatory matter, but finally Ridenhour found two young attorneys in Richmond, recent law school graduates, who agreed to take his case on a contingency basis.

I assumed the case would be settled out of court because there was no way Falwell would want his organization's dirty linen hung out for the whole world to see. As the court date drew near, it looked as if it would actually be tried. But the college flinched at the last moment—perhaps a week before the trial—and the word I heard was that they paid off heavily to avoid open litigation. Ridenhour told me in our last visit that he had won, but that a gag order had been part of the deal and he could not say anything more than that he had done "very well."

Someone later told me that he had received enough money from the settlement to buy three businesses and an airplane, and that he would never have to work again.

Recently, I Googled "Lynn Ridenhour" and got a Web site for "Dr. Lynn Ridenhour" of WinePress Ministries in Independence, Missouri. It gave a sketchy history of Ridenhour's life since his time in Lynchburg, indicating that he had earned a Ph.D. in writing at the University of Iowa and became a teacher at Brigham Young University in Utah. At some point, he had undergone a conversion to Mormonism while reading Joseph Smith's *Book of Mormon,* which is probably what led him to BYU. But his old proclivities for charismatic religion asserted themselves again and resulted in his termination there.

The plot thickens. Answering criticisms that (1) he had never taught at Liberty Baptist College, as he claimed, because authorities at the college denied his association there, and (2) he had written an article for *Penthouse* magazine about Liberty, Ridenhour provided evidence that he had indeed taught there, including phone numbers of people who could verify his story (one was Olga Kronmeyer), and then insisted that he had never written anything or intended to write anything for *Penthouse*.

I find this extremely curious, because I have in my possession, beside me as I write this, a copy of the article Ridenhour gave me, indicating that it was the one he had written for *Penthouse*. It is titled "A Professor's Two Years with Jerry Falwell," and it is a "first" typewritten copy, complete with occasional white-outs, on cream-colored Liberty Baptist College stationery, with a "Department of English" subheading and the names "Jerry Falwell, D.D., Chancellor, Founder" and "A. Pierre Guillermin, LL.D., President" printed at the bottom.

The article I have is thirty-six pages in length. On the last page, Ridenhour wrote, "I have learned some things these past two years":

Number One: Jerry Falwell's religion is not Christianity. There is no love in it.

Number Two: Fundamentalism is a sociological movement—not a religious movement that's moved by the "power of God." It's moved by the power of nationalism.

Number Three: Fundamentalism is the worst evil in America at the present: it poses as good "in the name of Christ."

Ridenhour said: "Three of us English professors are leaving at the end of this year. And all of us are leaving without jobs to go to." He described how difficult it was for Liberty Baptist College to find qualified teachers who were willing to come there. The departmental chair, he said, told him she had only twenty applications for six openings the following autumn. Another college in Lynchburg had received a thousand applications for a single opening. When the chair telephoned some people she really wanted to teach in the department, they laughed at her.

"I have kept the faith," Ridenhour concluded. "But now I must really trust the Lord. I need a job."

That was obviously before his suit against the college was settled out of court.

One thing was becoming very clear to me: there was more intrigue and mystery in the Falwell enterprises than anything I had ever known. I had lived for fifteen years in Nashville, the home base for three mainline Christian denominations, but the politics there never compared with the dynamic, ever-changing patterns of life in Lynchburg. Here was an umbrella organization with connections to groups all over America and a leader who was intimately linked to national politics, perhaps even to the underworld, and new information about them was coming to light virtually every day.

As busy as I was with my pastoral work, and as little time as I had to think about Jerry Falwell and the Moral Majority, I was constantly absorbing news and information about them all the time. Because Lynchburg was only an overgrown small town where business and family relationships crisscrossed like a tangle of Christmas-tree lights, very little happened that I didn't hear about, and of course reports ran the other way as well.

Jim Price was attached to our staff, as I have said, and we saw each other at least once or twice a week for staff meetings and worship services. We often did funerals together, and there would be time to talk as we robed or waited for the grieving family or rode to the cemetery. Jim kept me apprised of things that were going on with Falwell and his ministry—things that often didn't make it into the media. I regarded him and Bill Goodman as invaluable sources of information. They loved to gossip about Falwell but, for all their delight in sharing items of interest, were invariably as committed to accuracy as any two scholars could possibly be.

Falwell was certainly aware of their constant surveillance, and often took digs at them—as well as at me—in his remarks to the congregation at Thomas Road Baptist Church. On January 31, 1982, for example, at a service when he had Mrs. Francis Schaeffer as a guest, he mentioned that Price and Goodman had organized a program at Lynchburg College the week before in which an outside speaker had been brought in to address "the evils of Jerry Falwell and religious moralists."

"They're mad," he said, "because the book [*Jerry Falwell:*

An Unauthorized Profile] was a financial fiasco." He wondered where they got the money to bring in an outside
speaker, because "they only had eighty people show up." To
him, that was extremely small potatoes.

> "Dr. Price and Dr. Goodman," he continued, "are the two
> professors. Dr. Price is also an associate prof . . . at . . .
> uh . . . associate pastor at First Presbyterian Church where
> Dr. John Killinger is the pastor. And uh . . . it . . . you know,
> there's so many wonderful people at First Pres who really
> love God. I happen to know them. Many of them have
> come to me and apologized to me for their pastor and asso-
> ciate pastor and for their behavior. They really have. We have
> many of them support us financially in a heavy way.
>
> "And so I wanna say real quickly, don't ever think that
> the people at First Pres share the sentiments of their pastor
> and their associate pastor. Many of them do not. Some
> may, but many do not and really love the Lord and would
> never waste a penny of money or a minute of time to crit-
> icize another servant of God.
>
> "You know I feel that if we're out winning souls to
> Christ, building churches, doing the work of the king-
> dom, we just don't have time to rip at other preachers.
> That's why you've never heard me in twenty-five and a
> half years here criticize a preacher of the gospel. And I'm
> not going to start doing that now."

Talk about *occupatio,* the literary device of doing something while pretending not to!

"And, uh, Mrs. Schaeffer leaned over and quoted a verse to me that Paul wrote about 'Alexander the coppersmith had done me great harm, may the Lord reward him accordingly' (1 Timothy 1:20 and Acts 19:33). [*Laughter*] And I— ha, ha, ha, ha—I forgot, Paul did say that. Paul would fit here fine. [*Laughter*] But [*more laughter*], uh, I say all that so that you'll pray for them. The Scripture says that we should pray for those who despitefully use us. I hope you will pray for those two men and the pastor out at First Presbyterian, that God will move upon their hearts and cause somehow a real Christian love to begin flowing both ways, so that the cause of Christ is not injured by followers of Christ."

This was the kind of undercurrent that went on the whole time I lived in Lynchburg, not only from Falwell's pulpit but from the Lynchburg newspaper, which was fully in Falwell's pocket. His people kept up a steady barrage of letters to the editor, encouraged by his own frequent remarks about the "enemies" who were trying to bring him down. I was called "friend of Satan," "emissary of the devil," "Judas in the pulpit," and numerous other epithets deemed appropriate for anyone who dared to call the great evangelist into question.

My own members never answered. I'm not sure why they didn't. I never asked anyone. Maybe they thought I could take care of myself, or that I was only getting what I had asked for. Or maybe they were simply too polite in that decorous little town to write an editor about anything except in praise of the city's Christmas decorations or an exceptional concert by the Children's Chorale.

I'm inclined to think it was the latter reason. While we were in Lynchburg, the rector of St. John's Episcopal Church, the Reverend George Bean, retired. I liked George. He had been a navy chaplain before returning to civilian life and becoming a clergyman, and still had a kind of plainness and frankness about him from all those years in the military. As a fellow clergyman, I was invited to help roast George at a dinner in his church.

Because George had been pretty outspoken against Falwell and had shared with Jim Price and me the burden of those annual IRS audits, I decided to roast him in the most creative way I could. I borrowed a number of tape recordings of Falwell's sermons from Jim Price, listened to them, and fashioned an "interview" with Falwell in which I asked him questions about George Bean and Falwell answered in his own voice, with sentences from his sermons and extemporaneous remarks. An audiovisual expert in my congregation spent an evening with me excerpting and recording the selected responses from the tapes. Then, at the dinner, I asked the questions into the microphone at the head table and someone handling the tape machine played the responses.

It was really quite hilarious. For example, I asked, "Dr. Falwell, what would you say to George Bean as he prepares to retire?" Falwell's voice boomed out, "Whaddya wanna go and do that for?!" I said, "Dr. Falwell, do you have any advice about what George ought to do now that he's retiring?"

Again the big voice thundered, "All I can say is, if it feels good, *do* it!"

The dinner crowd was in stitches, and George had to wipe the tears from his eyes because he was laughing so hard.

But afterward a former Baptist minister who had become a banker and was a deacon in my church asked me to lunch, where he turned to me and said, very seriously, "John, you set our cause back by what you did."

"What do you mean, 'our cause'?" I asked.

"I mean with Falwell," he said.

I stared at him, not comprehending for a minute. Then it dawned on me. He thought the roast had been common and undignified, below the standards of polite Lynchburgers, which, to his mind, meant not stooping to a humorous broadside of the sort I had put together.

This time I was dignified, and did not tell him how I really felt about his reproach. *Our* cause, indeed! I had never noticed him, or anybody else in our congregation, for that matter, stepping up to bat for "our cause." They had never responded to attacks on their minister in the paper. They had merely stood by in silence, like the Christians in Nazi Germany.

I had always assumed they were cowards. But maybe it wasn't that at all. Maybe, to them and most of Lynchburg, it was a matter of dignity. And maybe they did feel that they were part of the "cause," even if they had said nothing and had never joined Jim Price and Bill Goodman and me on the firing line.

Looking back, I can see that this may have been true. It

may have been true because by that time public opinion about Falwell had begun to shift. Old Lynchburgers like my deacon friend had never taken a public stand against him and his burgeoning empire. But his popularity had reached its tipping point and begun to recede, even in Lynchburg.

All over town, and especially in the business community, there were complaints about Falwell. His church and college didn't pay their bills promptly. Sometimes they defaulted on them altogether. Contractors who had once been eager to work for him refused to return to the campus unless they were paid. The growing student body at Liberty Baptist College was posing problems for local welfare and health care budgets. There had been a court suit and a lot of flap over whether Falwell had to pay taxes on a shopping center his organization had acquired. He claimed it was church property, but others said no, it was business property and Falwell used it to make a profit. A restaurant in the shopping center served liquor, which offended many of Falwell's teetotaling supporters and made him look hypocritical.

A young woman who worked for the local newspaper had been frightened off after writing some articles critical of him, and a fresh young journalist named Darrell Laurant had taken her place as religion editor and was also raising questions about his operations.

Nationally, more and more books and articles pinpointed the famous preacher from Lynchburg as a fraud and a windbag. The editors of *Penthouse* and *Hustler* were regularly portraying him as a holy buffoon. *Hustler* ran a famous parody of a Campari ad featuring a fake interview with Falwell confessing he had once had incest with his mother in an outhouse while he was blind drunk. Ministers began to openly question both his motives and his theology. Organizations such as NOW and the ACLU regularly dubbed him a religious anachronism, a loudmouth preacher who thought of himself as the American pope.

And by the time of the 1984 elections, polls were beginning to show that Falwell's backing for a candidate in both state and national races had a negative effect, indicating that people everywhere were questioning whether this loud-mouthed preacher from Lynchburg should have a voice in how either Virginia or the nation was run. Politicians began distancing themselves from him, and he had to bootleg his influence by calling in markers and beseeching the faithful to elect his recommended candidates.

It was clear that his power was waning. His handlers were worried. Something had to be done to save the ailing power broker.

SIX

"Getting to Know You"

Robert "Bob" Snell was a handsome young realtor in Lynchburg who said that he was an atheist until he heard me preach. Bob's father was in the furniture business, and at first Bob worked with him. But they didn't get along well, so Bob studied to become a realtor. His pretty wife, Jo Anne, was a grade-school teacher and they had two attractive, well-behaved young sons. They were a beautiful family, but Bob and Jo Anne didn't seem to be entirely happy.

Maybe that's why Bob started coming to church. It wasn't long before he made a confession of faith and became an active participant in the life of the congregation.

He said he was a different man; and so did everybody else who had known him. He taught Sunday school, was elected to the diaconate, took part in the every-member canvass, worked with young people, and generally became an ardent church member.

He and Jo Anne invited my wife and me to dine in their home—Bob was a gourmet cook—and play tennis with them. He and I often played tennis alone. He was a fierce competitor and had a beautiful overhand smash. I admired his style and enjoyed watching the changes taking place in his life. I could tell he was toying with the idea of becoming a minister long before he announced that he had been called by God.

One day while this call was still materializing, Bob showed up in my office and announced, "Some of us have been talking, and we think it's a pity that you and Jerry Falwell go all over the country talking about one another and you don't even know one another."

I don't remember what I said. I probably cocked my head a little and merely smiled, wondering where this was going.

"Would you be interested in meeting with Falwell once a month so you could talk and get to know one another?"

So that was it! I knew Bob had become friends with Les Stone and George Stewart and some other men in the congregation who had been longtime Falwell supporters. They had decided that their pastor had become too visible an enemy of the local idol and wanted to pull his teeth.

It was a no-brainer for me. There was no way in aitch-eee-double-toothpicks Jerry Falwell was going to sit down with me. Not after the stuff that had passed between us for almost five years.

"Sure!" I said to Bob, feeling a little disappointed that he would be front man for a mission like this. "Falwell is probably the most interesting man in this town. I'd be glad to do it—if he wanted to."

I was counting on the fact that he wouldn't.

"Good!" said Bob, his face lighting up. "Falwell has already agreed!"

I felt inwardly foolish, as if I'd just fallen for a scam. It had been a setup! Not only that, it had probably originated not just with Bob and a handful of other Falwell supporters in my congregation, but with Falwell himself.

I would later learn that this was true, that Falwell had openly bragged to friends that he had begun a program of "neutralizing" his enemies. I was never sure who the other intended victims of his neutralization were. I don't think he made any overtures to Jim Price and Bill Goodman. George Bean had retired, so he wouldn't have been on the list. The other "enemies" must have lived in other places. As far as I know, I was the only local one.

But I had given my word, and I couldn't back down. I would have to go through with it.

Bob acted as intermediary for our first "date." Falwell and I were to meet for lunch at the Sheraton Inn, on his side of town. That was logical. There weren't any outstanding places on my side of town, and a meeting on my side would have caused a lot more commotion.

I left early, as I hadn't been to the Sheraton before and

didn't want to be late because I had to hunt for it. So I was the first to arrive. I checked the lobby and, when I didn't see him, stood at the front door and waited.

Falwell wheeled into the parking lot in a black SUV and rolled into a space opposite the front door. He was wearing his standard-issue dark suit and strode easily toward the hotel. He had a noticeable paunch, but was considerably thinner in those days than most people now remember him, and walked with the same energy that characterized everything else he did. His hair was still reasonably dark, turning salt and pepper, and a large shock bobbed at the edge of his forehead as he approached.

We smiled and shook hands. He spoke to someone at the desk and escorted me to the dining room, where the waiter knew him and became instantly deferential. It was a nice dining room, with white linen tablecloths and napkins to match. The silverware was heavier than that usually found in a hotel dining room. The waiter handed us menus and proceeded to fill our water glasses, pouring handily from the side of the pitcher so the ice would jostle out with the water.

Falwell laid his menu down the moment it was given to him, saying, "I know what I want!" It seemed appropriate. He always seemed to know what he wanted.

I was slower, and studied the menu for options.

"Try the crab-leg sandwich if you want something good," he said. "That's what I like."

I had never had a crab-leg sandwich, but his enthusiasm was catching. I closed my menu and said, "Great! I will!"

We made chitchat. I don't remember any of it now. I

only remember that it was a little awkward. It had been a bit easier that time in Les Stone's house because Les was there to moderate, or at least to fill in the chinks when the conversation lagged. Now we were on our own, and we probably both felt the pressure.

The sandwich was delicious. It wasn't real crab, I found out later, only faux crab. But it was really good. I followed Falwell's example and put ketchup on it. Later, I took other people to lunch there, and always recommended the crab-leg sandwich. And, following my example, they always doused their crab legs with ketchup.

By the end of the lunch that day, I wasn't relishing a repeat performance the next month. So I asked Falwell if he and his wife wouldn't come to our house for dinner one night. He said they would, but to call his secretary to set up the time. I did, and went home and told Anne about it.

"Oh gosh," she said, "what'll we have?"

I remember that dinner much better than I do the lunch. It was a good idea having it in our home with our wives present, because then we could talk about a lot of domestic things that made the conversation lighter and easier.

Macel Falwell was a pretty woman with beauty-parlor hair, a slightly broad face, and a thickening body. Falwell had met her in church, where she had been the pianist. He and his friend Jim Moon had gone to church that night—it was before he was converted—to find a couple of girls to go out with. One of them was Macel. At first, she was Moon's date, but later they switched. Meeting her and being converted changed Falwell's life. After his conversion, he left Lynchburg for the only time in his life to attend Baptist Bible College in Missouri. Then he came back, started Thomas Road Baptist Church with those dissident members from Park Avenue Baptist Church, Macel became his organist, and they married.

Anne and I had married young too, when I was barely nineteen and she had just completed high school. The two women had something to talk about. The Falwells had two sons and a daughter. We had two sons. More to talk about.

Anne remembers what she fixed for dinner that night. We began with spiced hot tomato juice and warm hors d'oeuvres—it was a cold night—in the living room. We ate by candlelight in the dining room—crab salad on avocado, an old family pork-chop dish with mushrooms and peas in a light tomato broth, mashed potatoes, and homemade rolls. Then, after dessert—a chocolate angel pie Anne had once been awarded a set of cookbooks for concocting—and coffee, we moved into the comfort of the den, where a fire was burning. Falwell sat in an easy chair on one side of the fireplace, and I took the chair on the other side. The two women sat on the sofa.

Macel was attending Liberty Baptist College. She hadn't had the opportunity of going to college when she was young. Now she couldn't get over the fact that she was making straight A's. "I didn't know I was so smart!" she giggled. I didn't mention something one of the Liberty professors had told me, that the year before, a physical education teacher there had reportedly been fired for giving Falwell's daughter Jeanie a B+ on her report card.

We talked about the Falwells' home on Smith Mountain

Lake, a favorite retreat spot for a lot of Lynchburgers, including our mutual friend George Stewart and his wife, who had a houseboat on the lake as well as a home on the shore. Macel encouraged Jerry to tell us about a joke he had recently played on their sons. He was happy to comply.

Jerry and Macel had been somewhere downstate below the lake and had stopped by the house on their way back to Lynchburg. The boys and their wives or girlfriends (I'm not sure if they were married then) were out on the lake somewhere, and were obviously in their bathing suits, because they had left their clothes in the bedrooms and their wallets were still in their pants. Seeing this, and not intending to wait for their return, Jerry took their wallets with him back to town and didn't leave a note to indicate that he and Macel had been there.

He and Macel had barely got home when the phone rang and one of the boys excitedly told them they had been robbed. Somebody had come into the house while they were on the lake and taken their billfolds and all their money, credit cards, and everything!

"What're you going to do?" asked Jerry. "Do you need me to bring you some money?"

"We called the sheriff," said the son, "and he and his deputies are on the case. But he didn't say if he thought they'd be able to catch whoever did it."

Jerry didn't confess right then. Instead, he hung up and phoned the sheriff's office to explain that it was a prank. Then he let his children stew a few hours before calling and telling them about the joke he had played on them.

"They didn't think it was funny," said Macel.

"I bet they didn't!" said Anne.

But Falwell was still obviously pleased with what he had done, and had another chuckle over it.

"He likes to play practical jokes," said Macel. "One time when he had been to Florida he brought a baby crocodile home with him on the plane and slipped it into our bathtub. I nearly died when I went in to take a bath and there was that—that ugly thing—flopping around in our tub!"

He laughed and she smiled at him. It was obvious that she still loved him as much as she had when they were youngsters and had just got married—maybe even more.

We chatted about this and that.

I asked how Falwell felt about the other TV evangelists. His immediate comment was, "Most of them won't last another ten years. Three of us will be left—Pat Robertson, Charles Stanley, and I will survive. But the rest will go under."

"Why will Robertson and Stanley survive?" I asked.

"Robertson's got a university and a satellite. Stanley has got a lot of rich backers down there in Georgia."

"What about Schuller?" I asked, amazed at this matter-of-fact attitude.

"Too thin," was his response. Thin? I supposed he meant that Schuller had no apparent undergirding theology, but I didn't question the judgment.

Later, when Falwell took over the *PTL Club* after Jim Bakker was arrested and put in prison, I wished I had thought to ask about him and Tammy, but I hadn't.

Macel remembered a story about Schuller and prompted

Jerry to tell it. He had been seated at a dinner in Florida next to Norman Vincent Peale and his wife, Ruth. In the course of their conversation, Falwell said to Peale, "What do you think of the way Robert Schuller has adopted your old theme of positive thinking?" Peale was polite, he said. He picked up his water glass, took a sip, and replied, "They say imitation is the sincerest form of flattery."

At this, Falwell said, Ruth Peale leaned across her husband and hissed, "I think he's awful!"

Both the Falwells laughed.

I commented on a huge diamond ring Falwell was wearing. It caught the light and flashed animatedly every time he moved his hand a certain way.

"One of his fans sent him that," said Macel proudly.

"Oh?" I said.

"I don't usually wear it," said Falwell. "I just had it appraised the other day and haven't put it away."

"The jeweler said it's worth ten thousand dollars!" said Macel.

"Wow," I think I intoned.

"People are always sending him gifts," she said. "He has a drawer full of things like that."

"Do you ever sell them?" I asked.

He studied the ring and said, "Sometimes." He was clearly embarrassed to talk about it. I let the matter drop.

One thing I learned during our conversation about his busy schedule was that the Moral Majority had hired some people to serve as his trainers. He was supposed to meet with them every morning to go over news developments and rehearse what he was supposed to say about them. The organization was clearly trying to head off the kind of gaffes for which he had become famous. I received the impression that he didn't really like this clamp on his spontaneity, but accepted it because the gaffes usually cost them so much money from donors and so much effort to repair.

Once or twice, I tried to steer the conversation toward theological matters, but it was obvious that neither of them felt comfortable about that. I sensed again what I had sensed in Les Stone's dining room months before, that Falwell was genuinely insecure around people whose education was more extensive than his. I didn't want to embarrass him, so I let it drop. I think even Anne was more comfortable when I did.

It was funny, now that I look back on it, the four of us sitting there together that evening. We had had such similar backgrounds—we had all grown up in the Baptist faith, had married young, had had little Baptist churches to pastor, and had had so many rich experiences since. Falwell had worked hard and had single-handedly, almost, built a great evangelical empire right there in his hometown. I, on the other hand, had moved on from my Baptist beginnings, had earned a Ph.D. in literature, gone to Harvard Divinity School, become a teacher, lived overseas on several occasions, and was now the pastor of a Presbyterian church. Instinctively, I wanted to bridge the gap between us, to identify with them in the things where we could really understand one another and be lasting friends.

If Falwell had been telling the truth, that he had set out

to neutralize his enemies, it had worked. I would have to be less hard on him now that I knew him better, now that he and Macel had sat at our table with us and then visited for a couple of hours in our den. I had tried never to attack him personally, only his methods of ministry and the theology he espoused, which I found objectionable in a man as influential as he was. Now I would have to be even more careful in how I talked about him, because I wouldn't want to hurt a friend's feelings.

It was in the spirit of friendship, a couple of weeks later, that we went to St. Paul's Episcopal Church in downtown Lynchburg to hear Falwell as the inaugural speaker in a community Lenten series on the general subject of peace. I was to be the last speaker, a few weeks later, and wanted to hear what he would say because he had been making a lot of militant remarks about America and the Soviet Union. If he preached about peace the reporters would probably hold him accountable for all those remarks about America's role in the world, especially vis-à-vis the USSR.

He solved that problem by totally ignoring the assignment and talking about salvation instead.

St. Paul's was not a large church, and Falwell, with his larger-than-life presence, seemed to overflow the chancel with volume and enthusiasm. He didn't turn them up in order to impress the crowd. He was simply being himself, which normally called for a larger space in which to operate.

Anne and I had sat eight or ten pews from the front, on the "epistle" side of the church, as Anglicans say, where we had a clear view of the pulpit and could easily communicate our presence to Falwell. That seemed somehow to be important in our new relationship.

When the final hymn had been sung and the benediction pronounced by the local rector, the organist began playing a soft, undemonstrative postlude. Falwell came striding down from the chancel toward the pews, waving at us and shouting, so that everyone in the building stopped talking to listen, "Anne! John! Come go to England with me!"

We had no idea what he was talking about, but we found this unusual show of camaraderie between two parties that had until of late been regarded as mortal enemies extremely embarrassing, and wished we could have sunk under the pews.

Instead of coming all the way up to us before explaining, Falwell began talking to us in his stentorian voice from the edge of the first pew. He held a packet of papers aloft as part of the explanation. "I've got a bunch of first-class tickets here on American Airlines. I know you like England. Come and go with us!"

Of course we had everybody's undivided attention. But fortunately, by the time he had said this, Falwell had caught up with us in our own pew, where he continued the explanation. President Reagan had sent the tickets. He wanted Falwell to go to England to debate Robert Menzies, the prime minister of New Zealand, at the Oxford English Speaking Club on the deployment of nuclear forces in NATO. He could take along anybody he wanted. From the look of the wad of tickets, I thought he could take at least a dozen people!

"What do you know about nuclear arms and NATO?" I asked.

"Nothing!" Falwell chirped, undaunted. "Somebody'll brief me on the way over."

"When are you going?" asked Anne.

"Tonight," he said. "Can you go along?"

Anne looked at me. She was always ready to go to England.

I smiled and said, "I'll have to check my calendar. I'm afraid I have a wedding Saturday, though."

"Can't you get somebody else to take it?"

"Not if it's who I think it is. But I'll check as soon as I get back to the church and call you, okay?"

Anne and I drove home, amazed. After we'd had a bite of lunch, I went back to the church and looked at my desk calendar. Sure enough, I did have a wedding on Saturday, and it was the daughter of some people I wouldn't disappoint for the world. I telephoned Jerry's office and told his secretary to say I was very grateful for the invitation, but I did have a wedding I couldn't get out of and we wouldn't be able to go.

Later that afternoon, Anne took a phone call at home. "Jerry," the voice on the other end of the line said. "I got John's message. Sorry he can't go. Macel's decided she's not going either. She's not keen about flying. Anne, why don't you come on and go with me? We'll have a ball!"

I would give a lot to have overheard Anne's answer. She said she stuttered and stammered, trying to think of what to say. What she was really thinking was, "Boy, wouldn't that give people something to talk about, me getting off a plane

in London and walking by all those reporters with Jerry Falwell!" She made some excuse about not wanting to go overseas without her husband, and Falwell eventually accepted
that as her answer.

She could hardly wait to tell me when I got home that
evening.

"Imagine!" she said. "This town would never have been
the same!"

Indeed it wouldn't.

We had one more meeting with the Falwells, a few weeks
later. We might have extended our get-togethers for a year
or more, and wound up being good friends, but for the in-
tervention of the First Congregational Church of Los Angeles, which asked me again to become their senior minister,
following the five-year pastorate of Dr. Donald Ward, the
minister they had called when I turned them down in 1980.

True to his word that they would try again when Dr. Ward
retired, Thomas Hunter Russell, the flamboyant Hollywood
attorney who had chaired the search committee in 1980, telephoned the Sunday afternoon after Ward announced his retirement and asked if I would consider coming. By this time,
after almost six years in Lynchburg, I think I would have said
yes if the invitation had been to Timbuktu!

Russell's call came a few days after the beginning of
Lent. Anne and I flew to Los Angeles in early April 1986 to
talk to the new search committee. My father died later that
month in Kentucky, and Anne and I drove down to bury

him. While we were on that trip, we made the decision to leave Lynchburg and move to Los Angeles. It seemed to both of us the thing to do.

The funeral had forced us to postpone one planned engagement with Jerry and Macel, and we were happy to accept another. They invited us to meet them for dinner on Saturday evening at Crown Sterling, a favorite steak house on their side of town, and go with them from there to the spring concert at Liberty Baptist College. I said I was afraid we couldn't come as early as we needed to because I had a wedding that Saturday afternoon and wouldn't be able to get away before five-thirty or six. Jerry said that was okay, just to get there when we could.

I've always been concerned about being punctual, and was worried about our timing that evening. The concert started at seven-thirty. Granted, the distance from the restaurant to the campus would take only ten minutes or so to cover. But when Anne and I hit some traffic and didn't get to the restaurant until ten after six, I was nervous.

"Don't worry," said Jerry, who was on the phone when we walked in, talking to somebody at the college. "I've just sent word for Guillermin to prolong the introductions, if necessary. We've got plenty of time."

They had already been given a nice table at the side of the room where we weren't crowded by other diners, and the waiters had been alerted to the fact that we would need to be served as promptly as possible.

Jerry and Macel knew what they wanted without looking at the menu. They ate there at least once a week, and favored the tenderloin steaks. Anne and I decided to go with their preference and said to bring us the same.

The service *was* prompt. Our salads, bread, and iced tea appeared almost at once. Jerry and Macel ate their steaks when they arrived with casual ease, as if we had lots and lots of time. Anne and I ate ours with reasonable dispatch, wanting to finish by the time they did.

I sneaked several peeks at my watch. Six-forty-five. Six-fifty-five. Seven-oh-five. Thank goodness, we were all through eating at seven-fifteen, and in anticipation of a quick exit, I began to edge my chair backward.

The waiter came to our table.

"You all will have some coffee, won't you?" asked Jerry.

"Uh," I hesitated, "do you think we really have time?" Translated, that meant, "Hadn't we better get on our way?"

"Aw, sure," said Jerry, tossing his hand in the air as if dismissing any thought about the time. "I know Macel wants her dessert, don't you, Macel?"

I looked at Macel. She was relaxed, in no hurry. "Oh yes," she said. "It comes with the meal."

"Bring us all dessert and coffee," said Jerry to the waiter.

The dessert, we learned, was strawberry parfait. Macel loved it, and got it every time she came to Crown Sterling.

I raised my arm as if stretching and sneaked a look at my watch. The coffee was just being poured, the desserts were yet to appear, and it was already seven-twenty-five. I resigned myself. We couldn't possibly make it now. Just relax and go along with the Falwells, I said to myself. They're in charge here, we aren't.

I thought Macel would never finish her dessert. She clanked her long-handled spoon down in the bottom of the glass until every smidgeon of the parfait was gone. I half expected her to stick her finger in the glass and lick that.

At last, Falwell signaled the waiter to bring the bill. He signed it with a flourish and we all began scooting back to stand up.

Anne whispered to me, "I need to go to the bathroom before we leave!" Almost in midwhisper, we heard Macel say, "Let's stop by the restrooms on our way out. We may be a while at the concert."

It was well after eight o'clock when we arrived at the campus music center. Falwell's attendants were waiting when we drove up. We got out and they whisked the car off to wherever they parked it. We were only a few feet from the door of the large brick building we entered.

The auditorium was built like a Roman theater, with ramps running down from the top tier to the stage at the bottom. It was a long way down and the place was packed with people, most of them parents, relatives, and friends of the students taking part in the various musical numbers. I had the feeling they were very restless from the long wait.

I knew Pierre Guillermin was even more nervous. He had been onstage for more than half an hour, doing everything but tap dance to keep the people entertained while they waited for Chancellor Falwell.

Jerry and Macel swept down the ramp like the King and Queen of England. Anne and I followed, feeling sheepish and ashamed that we had had a part in making all these people wait. Our escort led us to four empty seats in the middle of the front row, right before the stage. I half expected the crowd to rise in a giant ovation of some kind, but Guillermin was still talking.

When we had taken our seats, Falwell looked jovially up at the poor, exhausted president and said, "We're here, Pierre! You can begin!" And with that, Guillermin finished a sentence, turned the stage over to the director of the evening's performance, and sank into the darkness as the house lights faded and the stage lights came on.

I don't remember a single thing the choirs and soloists sang or played that night. I'm sure everything was first class. Music was something Liberty Baptist College excelled at, even before it had built its top-notch sports teams. But my nerves were shot from the tension of having done a wedding, rushed over to the restaurant, worried about getting out of there and to the concert on time, and then strode down the ramp behind the Falwells. I wanted to collapse inside myself and not have to speak or respond to anything until the concert was over.

I only remember one other thing from the evening. When we were standing with the Falwells after the concert, speaking to various people who came up to Jerry, he put his arm around Anne's waist at one point and was gently hugging her when she disengaged his arm and said sweetly, "You thought I was Macel, didn't you?" It was obvious that he was sweet on her, and I thought she had handled the matter with admirable tact.

I remember somebody's defining "tact" many years ago,

and saying how it is different from mere politeness. Imagine, said the person, a man opens a door to the restroom and there is a lady sitting on the toilet. It would be *polite* of him to step back and close the door, saying, "I'm so sorry, madam, I didn't realize there was someone in here!" But it would be *tactful* of him to step back and close the door while muttering, "Sorry, sir, I didn't know this was occupied!"

Anne had plainly responded with tact!

Bob Snell, incidentally, did become a minister. He earned his way through Union Theological Seminary in Richmond by working as a waiter on the weekends, when he came home from his dormitory room to be with his family. He did so admirably in his course work, and became such a capable preacher, that his very first assignment, out of seminary, was to be the associate pastor of tony Brick Presbyterian Church in New York City.

From there he became pastor of a church of his own in northern New Jersey, and then, after a few years in that position, he was called to a large church in Lincoln, Nebraska. I telephoned him recently to ask how he and Jo Anne were doing. It was a Saturday afternoon and they were preparing to leave for a party in one location and then a wedding in another.

They seemed to be very happy in Nebraska. I asked if they had been back to Lynchburg recently. Yes, Bob said, he had flown to Richmond for a celebration for one of his old professors who was leaving and had gone on to Lynchburg for a visit while he was in the vicinity. The date of his visit appeared to correspond with the time when Falwell died and I asked if that had been the case.

"As a matter of fact," said Bob, "I heard the announcement of his death as I was driving into Lynchburg."

Then Bob recalled the time he had been the go-between to bring Falwell and me together. I asked him how well he knew Falwell. The only time he had ever been near him, he said, was when he was arranging for the rendezvous between us. I smiled to myself, and wondered how it had all happened.

My guess is that Falwell telephoned George Stewart or Les Stone, and George or Les began talking to Bob about getting the two of us together, and then Bob was given the job of making it happen.

I didn't ask him about it. I'd rather keep it as a mystery.

SEVEN

The Gum on My Shoe
That Wouldn't Go Away

As much as Anne and I both wanted to begin a new episode of our lives in sunny Los Angeles, leaving Lynchburg was not easy. We had built a home of our own design there and had put down a lot of roots in a relatively few years. I had married and buried many people, and we had become intricately involved with a host of wonderful folks, including our Birthday Club, a group of couples about our age who got together for dinner once a month at one of our homes.

With my father's demise in April 1986, my parents were both gone, but Anne still had her father and four siblings in

Kentucky and Tennessee. Our older son, who married a girl from Pittsburgh, was in seminary in Richmond, and our younger son, who had just graduated from college, was engaged to a girl in Alexandria, Virginia, and had just taken a job in Washington, D.C. We would be moving across country from everybody we were kin to and most of the landmarks dear and familiar to us.

I have never moved well, as I indicated in my sermon when I came to Lynchburg, "Jesus and the Terror of Moving." Even though I could wax rhapsodic about "a new beginning" and getting away from the kind of deep involvements that begin sucking a pastor down after four or five years in the same location, I began having night sweats about going. My diary for this period is filled with brooding reflections of this anxiety.

One night I had an eerie dream that to this day I can still recall quite vividly. I looked up into the sky and saw a large plane flying very low overhead. A plume of smoke was issuing from its prow and it was losing altitude. Behind it followed another plane, only slightly smaller than the first. On either side of the larger plane flew two smaller planes as escort. I remember saying, "They're *our* planes." It was as if there had been some kind of apocalyptic war and our side had lost. These were our planes limping home after the battle. The sight filled me with deep, unexplainable remorse. It seemed to say that everything was lost and the world was empty.

Pondering the dream, I wrote in my diary what it might mean. Perhaps the larger plane, with the smoke billowing from it, was me. I was wounded and drifting away from the battle. The slightly smaller plane was my wife. The two escort fighters were our sons.

One can never be absolutely certain about the meanings of such dreams, but my interpretation still seems fitting. My fight in Lynchburg was over. I wasn't destroyed, but I was wounded, and I was coasting away toward safety. Anne was faithfully following me. Our sons weren't going to California with us, but they were always there. We could count on them when we needed to.

Our last weeks in Lynchburg were exceptionally busy. There were so many people to see, so many good-byes to say. I tried to wrap up all the business I had been taking care of for the church, and to make sure the staff would be able to carry on efficiently in my absence. We flew to Los Angeles again to look for a home. The church was willing to buy us a parsonage, but wanted us to choose the one we wanted. There were lots of things we wanted to leave behind and not carry across the country. I gave many cartons of books to an African-American seminary, and we hauled several small truckloads of furniture and yard equipment to a family that had taken bankruptcy and was having yard sales to get back on their feet. We sold the home we had built. The church gave us a going-away party and presented us with gifts, and we went to dinner with the Birthday Club at a favorite restaurant.

We gave ourselves two weeks past my leaving the church to get everything packed—we wanted to do our own china and keepsakes and my books and papers. On the Sunday morning after we had left the church, we were hard at work when the phone rang. The young woman weeping on the line was one I had counseled a few weeks earlier when she and her husband, the son of some prominent church members, were having marital problems. Her husband had just come back from a business trip and confessed his infidelity. They had been up all night. Could I come over?

I tried to beg off. I was no longer their pastor. This was a matter for one of the staff members or somebody else who would be around long enough to see it through.

"Please," she begged. "Please." There was a tone of utter desperation in her voice.

So I rinsed my face and hands, combed my hair, and drove to their house. The morning service was still going on at First Presbyterian Church. The young woman was confused and despondent. Her husband was broken up and almost incoherent.

I talked to him about his life and his faith. He had been a member of the church since he was a boy, and his parents had held all kinds of offices in it. But he admitted he had never been truly converted, had never really given his heart to Christ. We talked about it for a while and he said he would like to do it now, he wanted to turn his life over to Jesus, give up the woman he had been seeing, and save his marriage.

His wife was still in shock from the revelation that he had been with the woman while on his business trip. She wasn't sure she wanted to save the marriage. It would take time, she said; she needed to think, to wait, to let things take their course for a while.

In a sudden inspiration, I thought of Bob Snell. Bob and Jo Anne had had some tensions of their own a few years ago. He was now a strong, stalwart Christian. Moreover, he was personable and capable of leading this couple through this difficult passage in their marriage.

I said to them, "I have a friend. You know him very well. I am going to ask him to be your counselor for the next few weeks. May I tell him your story and ask him to come to see you this afternoon?"

They looked at each other. The young man appeared to be on the verge of a breakdown. They looked at me and nodded.

That afternoon I called Bob. He was hesitant, but said he would do it. He went to see the couple within the hour, and spent most of the afternoon talking with them. He became their faithful therapist and helped them through the pain and confusion.

Several years later, when Anne and I moved back to Virginia, we went to First Presbyterian Church on a Sunday morning to visit. Someone tapped me on the shoulder and I looked around. It was that couple, sitting right behind us. They were radiantly happy, and thought it was providential that they should see me and be able to tell me.

Bob had done a wonderful job, even before becoming a minister!

I did one monumentally stupid thing before I left Lynchburg. Bruce Thomson, a fine man who was head of a

Coca-Cola Bottling Company plant and a member of First
Presbyterian's session, asked, on the night I handed in my
resignation, if I would please write a paper or preach a sermon on why the church's ministers all seemed to leave so
soon after arriving. My immediate predecessor, a bright
young pastor named Timothy Croft, had stayed only two
years before going to a large church in Florida. The pastor
before him, Dr. Jerold Shetler, had stayed four years and
gone to a large church in Texas. The one before that, Dr.
Herbert Barks, also stayed only four years.

I knew there was a lot of concern about this rapid turn-
over, and, being a teacher as well as a pastor, wanted to honor
Bruce's request by giving a thoughtful answer. I considered
doing it in a sermon, but didn't feel that was appropriate
during a worship service. So I decided to write a white
paper on the subject and duplicate it for anyone who wanted
a copy.

It was one of the biggest mistakes I ever made as a pastor!

First, I got too creative. There were two sides to many of
the things I needed to say, and I decided to offer them by
making the paper a dialogue. I called the two speakers in the
dialogue J-1 and J-2, the two sides of my own personality, so
they could speak to one another. That was too flippant, too
artsy, for a lot of my members.

Second, I was too serious about the assignment and revealed thoughts about the Lynchburg pastorate that were
simply too hard for some people to take. They were in
mourning that their pastor was leaving, and instead of merely
putting my arms around them and crying with them, I was

telling them why ministers didn't always feel comfortable in their church.

What I told them, in essence, was that their search committees had been too thorough, doing nationwide searches to find the most exciting, dynamic pastors they could identify, and had convinced these young men—at forty-seven, I had been the oldest—to come to one of the most isolated towns in America, where they had a difficult time adjusting to local mores and conventions. Lynchburg's largely ingrown population, moreover, invariably treated anyone who hadn't been born there as an outsider, making it hard for ministers and their families to feel truly loved and accepted. And, I confessed, there was the added problem of the city's being the heart of the Falwell enterprises—*OTGH,* Liberty Baptist College, and the Moral Majority—which skewed the entire religious sensibility of the area and made the average pastor in the community feel like the odd person out.

I tried not to be critical of Lynchburgers—one of my two personae was always raising the other side of every matter and reminding its alter ego of the many good things about life in their community—but I think I made 90 percent of my members at least partially unhappy with my comments. Ten percent of them clapped me on the back and said it was exactly what should have been said, and that they had been waiting for someone to say it. The others, though, were so hurt to think I could even express such feelings that it cast a tangible pall over our final days and activities in the church.

I'm reporting this, painful as it is, because there is a reason for it that will presently become apparent.

Our trip across the country was pleasant, and Anne and I felt relieved and stronger once we had crossed the Mississippi and were rolling toward California. There were a couple of downers on the other end. The house the church had purchased was flea-infested—so badly that the carpets had to be pulled up and new ones installed. And our movers failed to remove about forty cartons of books from the hold of the van until they were discovered, two weeks later, after the van had been washed and the books were ruined. But we felt relief to be out of Lynchburg and drawing a new line under our lives so we could start over with a new ministry, a new congregation, and a sprawling, challenging new city.

Our first Sunday in the vast sanctuary of First Congregational Church was breathtaking. Lloyd Holzgraf, the organist, was the finest we had ever heard. Dr. Thomas Somerville, the minister of music, had one of the largest, most magnificently disciplined choirs we could imagine. The liturgy, from the long procession at the beginning to the majestic recessional at the end, was soaring and uplifting. And getting to preach from the high, ornately carved pulpit to a great crowd of upturned faces, reaching back so far that I couldn't even identify them beyond the middle of the nave, would have been a thrill to the most jaded preacher!

We had been in Los Angeles only a few weeks, and were just getting settled into some routines and learning to find our way around the metropolis, when my office took a phone call from someone at the *Michael Jackson Show* in Hollywood. This particular Michael Jackson was a sixtyish, puckish little man, originally from South Africa, who had for several years been the host of a nationally syndicated radio show that was just being taken to television. He had read about me in the papers, the representative said, and would like to interview me for his TV program. The secretary who had taken the message, Nancy Huddleston, had been in and out of show business most of her life, having got her start years before as a young ingénue on the Arthur Godfrey show, and she was excited about the publicity this would generate for the church. I told her to call them back and tell them I'd do it.

Tony Curtis, the actor, was sitting in the studio waiting room when I arrived. He was there to promote some new movie on Jackson's show, and was scheduled to go on just before I did. I was amazed at how old and jaded he looked, and at the fact that he was clad in old jeans, a black shirt, and canvas boat shoes. He was also as nervous as a cat, and continually got up and sat down, got up and paced the room, then sat down again. We chatted briefly before he was called in for makeup, but I can't remember anything we said.

When I entered the studio after my own slight encounter with a makeup assistant, Jackson was smoking a cigarette and drinking from a coffee cup during a series of ads. He was exchanging cryptic remarks with one of the stagehands. I was impressed by his markedly clipped British accent and the short, staccato-like sound bursts in which he spoke. As I took my chair and was being miked, he said hello and told me he wanted to talk with me about fundamentalism.

"Oh no," I said to myself. I thought I had put that behind me.

When the programming resumed, Jackson talked even more rapidly than before. He said that I was the new senior minister at the First Congregational Church, the city's oldest English-speaking congregation, and that I had come to L.A. from Lynchburg, Virginia, home of the Reverend Jerry Falwell and the Moral Majority. Almost without further ado, he fired at me: "What is it about fundamentalism to which you object?"

He had warned me, but I wasn't prepared for such an abrupt entry into the subject. I don't remember exactly what I said, but I'm sure I stammered out something about fundamentalism being some people's attempt to restore a form of Christian faith that had never really existed except in their own minds.

"What was it like to live in Lynchburg, Virginia, the home of Jerry Falwell and the *Old-Time Gospel Hour*?" he asked. "Mr. Falwell certainly doesn't look at the world the way you do. Did you have to pay a price for believing as you do?"

Ah, I thought, he's obviously after a shot of drama because he's fighting for ratings and wants his show to be as memorable as possible. I was tempted to say no and force him into another line of questioning.

Instead, I recited some of the things that had happened to us—the death warnings, the tapped phone lines, the abortive

garbage collections, the diverted mail, harassment by the
IRS. As before, I was careful not to directly implicate Falwell himself, and took pains to point out that he had a large
organization and probably couldn't control everything his
associates did.

I think the interview consumed about fifteen minutes,
including a commercial break in the middle. Then, at the
very end of the segment, Jackson said, "Be sure and tune in
tomorrow, when our guest will be the Reverend Mr. Jerry
Falwell himself! We'll see what Mr. Falwell has to say!"

Jackson told me as I wiped off my makeup that Falwell
was in Anaheim to speak to a religious educators' convention and he thought it would be interesting to have us on his
program on succeeding days. I didn't know what to say. I
had been had! I think I raised my eyebrows and shook my
head as the program director gave him a one-minute warning to get back in his chair.

I felt disappointed as I left, and vaguely angry at being
tricked. Tony Curtis was still there, lounging around the
guest area outside. He had watched the program from there,
and said something like, "Great job, pastor!" I thanked him.
"I'm Catholic myself," he said as I let myself out the door,
"but maybe I'll catch your act sometime!"

As far as I know, he never did.

I drove back to the church and spent the rest of the day
laboring at my usual rock pile. Anthony Chierichetti, the
genial sound man at our church whose personally favorite
claim to fame was having worked with the sound team on

Walt Disney's *Fantasia,* stopped by my office later in the afternoon to give me an audiotape of the Michael Jackson program he had recorded.

"It was great!" he said.

Anthony was always encouraging.

I don't think I watched the *Michael Jackson Show* the next day—I can't remember doing so—but Anne did. So did a lot of the older women in our church, because they had watched their pastor the preceding day and wanted to see the follow-up. But Anthony made an audiotape of this program too and brought it by my office. I was shocked at what I heard.

Jackson wasted no time. He said he had the Reverend Dr. Jerry Falwell on the phone with him—not there in person as he had intimated the day before—and began to enact a charade he and Falwell had apparently cooked up together. He pretended not to know Falwell was in Anaheim—once he even asked if he were speaking from Lynchburg, Virginia—and inquired whether Falwell had seen his show the day before. Falwell said he hadn't, but that one of his friends—"someone in support of our ministry"—had taped the program and sent him the tape, so he had listened to it.

Jackson asked what he thought of it. Falwell began at once to disparage the things I had said about our garbage being picked up before the regular collection, our telephone being tapped, and our mail being stolen, patronizingly chuckling as he responded to these charges and saying there was "absolutely no truth" in them. He didn't mention the death threats or our problem with the IRS.

"Dr. Killinger left First Presbyterian Church under pressure," he continued, "and the people of First Presbyterian were quite happy when he left. He wrote a very harsh letter to the press when he left, and to the people."

Jackson stopped him abruptly, saying he wanted to play a brief clip from my remarks the day before. In the clip, Jackson asked me about Falwell's technique as a preacher, and I mentioned in my response that Falwell and other fundamentalist preachers regularly used paranoia as a tool for exploiting people and gaining their support.

"You've heard Dr. Killinger," Jackson said in his crisp, rapid-fire way. "Now, Mr. Falwell, what do you say to that?"

"John and Anne Killinger," replied Falwell, "are very bright people and very fine Christians." I had said a lot of bad things about him, he reported, but I had "felt badly about them" and Anne and I had invited him and his wife to dinner at our house. They had come and had a lovely evening. I apologized for my behavior, he said, and he "felt that any jealousy or critical spirit had been healed." "But then suddenly under pressure he left there and wrote a very harsh letter to his church—he was going out to Charlton Heston's church, wherever that is, is it in Hollywood?"

Jackson said, "No, it's in Los Angeles."

"It sounds like," said Falwell, "he was very bitter, I know, towards his church, his membership. It's like he's had an emotional breakdown. I hope that's not the case."

Jackson next asked him about the badgering tactics I had said some of the *Old-Time Gospel Hour* ministers used to get people in the psychiatric ward of the hospital to sign over their social security checks and property deeds. Falwell laughed—again patronizingly—and said that was "totally false, of course, and John knows that," because no hospital would permit that to happen even if the ministers had wanted to do such a thing. "John's not given to lying *usually.*" (He emphasized the word "usually.") There were two hospitals in Lynchburg, he said, and the administrators of both were good friends of his. Jackson could check with them if he liked.

"I'm sorry John's filled with bitterness," he continued, on a roll, "and I'm afraid it will affect the success of his ministry here. He failed in Lynchburg and he's setting himself up for a failure here with that kind of bitterness and dishonesty."

At this point, Jackson took a call from a man who identified himself as a clinical psychologist and said he had a question for Falwell. He had many patients, as psychologist friends of his did, he said, who were deeply disturbed by their experiences with fundamentalism. He would like Falwell to comment on that.

Falwell's immediate response, without a moment's hesitation, was to ask if the man was from Fundamentalists Anonymous. He had had a similar question recently from a man who identified himself as belonging to that group. Jackson asked the man if he was a member of such a group, and the man said he was. Falwell then spoke dismissively of the caller, saying he "probably is not a clinical psychologist" and that there are a lot of "bitter people out there" who want to take issue with people who love God and preach the Gospel. Fundamentalists Anonymous, he said, acts "like believers are all mentally ill. Billy Graham isn't mentally ill."

(This was a skillful rejoinder. He was trading on Graham's popularity with the average listener.)

Moving on, Jackson played another clip from my conversation the day before in which he asked what I thought was the worst thing about TV evangelism as practiced in this country. I replied that I regretted the way it misrepresented Christianity and betrayed millions of uncritical viewers into assuming that its distorted version was the only authentic one.

When Jackson asked Falwell to respond to these remarks, Falwell said once again that I was nursing "a very deep bitterness," and repeated that "John and Anne befriended Macel and me and apologized before they left Lynchburg." There was "a big row at First Presbyterian Church," he said, and I had written a letter saying "I'm leaving this church because it seems to be more in line with Jerry Falwell's theology than with mine." I had deeply hurt everybody, he claimed, and deserted them in their woundedness.

Jackson played one last clip of my remarks, a kind of summary statement in which I said—once more responding to what he had asked—that most TV evangelists debased the sense of what Christianity is really about, their programs were often in poor taste, and, because of their venal motivations, they were actually committing sacrilege in the name of religion.

Again Falwell linked himself to Billy Graham and Charles Stanley—he must have regarded the three of them as the trinity of great modern evangelists—and said it was "very rude" of me to attack these servants of God the way I did. Once more he said that I had apologized to him in Lynchburg, but that now I had come three thousand miles away and reverted to form. A good friend of Falwell's, he said, "a member of Dr. Killinger's church, I think the chairman of his board, told me that he came to Lynchburg trying to get some notoriety by attacking TV ministers, and it didn't work and it cost him his pulpit, and I guess he's probably on his way to learning the same thing in Southern California."

One more time he emphasized that I was having a nervous breakdown and was lying about everything. He said it was very sad. But my wife, Anne, he said, was not like me. "Anne's very different from John," he declared. "She's a real honey!"

Anne cried as she watched. She couldn't believe a nationally known Christian leader—even Jerry Falwell— would say the things he was saying about her husband, all patently false, and she was mortified at his paying her such a cheap, offhanded compliment.

For my part, when I listened to the tape, I was amazed at the breezy way Falwell had turned off all my criticisms of fundamentalism and TV evangelists with ad hominem attacks on me. For the record, everything he said was false. I had not had a breakdown. I was not bitter. I did not fire off an angry letter to the press, or to my church. I did not say my people were theologically more akin to him than to me. And I did not apologize to him. Not once, not ever.

It isn't that I can't find it in myself to admit error and offer apologies; I often do. But I had never attacked Falwell personally, as he had me, and I never believed I had done anything for which I ought to apologize.

My mind reverted to my experience with the Southern Baptist Sunday School Board in Nashville, many years before, and the way the board's executive secretary had spread the word that I had apologized for the things I had said about the board in my address to students at Golden Gate Baptist Theological Seminary, and that I had publically wept and been forgiven at some mythical banquet I was supposed to have attended. Was there a sort of manual for handling these occasions that I wasn't aware of? Had Falwell and the executive secretary been aware of some standard operating procedure for deflecting criticism?

I found it interesting, years later, when Jim Bakker accused Falwell of stealing the *PTL Club* from him, that Falwell responded by saying that Bakker "either has a terrible memory, or is very dishonest, or he is emotionally ill."* Apparently this was SOP for Falwell. I can only wonder how many times he used it in defending himself against his enemies.

Anne had barely turned off the TV after Michael Jackson's show when the phone rang. It was a miserable old church member named Kay Chandler, who sang in the choir, had her hand in half the organizations in the church, and was known by everyone as an insufferable, outspoken meddler.

"Is it true?" Kay demanded in her customarily abrasive

Time, June 24, 2001.

tone. "Did your husband have an emotional breakdown? Did he have to leave his last church?"

A few days later, I received a letter from Falwell. He was still on the offensive, and asked why I was continuing to tell lies about him. He was very disappointed in me, he said, and he knew I was a great disappointment to Anne as well. Again I was amazed that he had such unmitigated gall that he could behave to me, who knew the facts, as if he had been speaking truthfully on Jackson's program.

Suddenly I knew Falwell better as an enemy than I had ever known him before. I realized he would go to any length, say anything that popped into his head, to turn an unfavorable situation around. He must have had to do it all the time, to affect the stance of the injured party in order to deflect people away from whatever truth was being revealed about him. I knew he was a street fighter, but even some street fighters have ethical standards. Jerry Falwell, I decided, didn't.

When I showed the letter to Anne, she said, "I want to answer him. Do I have your permission?"

I laughed. "Since when," I asked, "have you needed that?"

"I mean it," she said. "Is it all right if I tell him exactly what I think?"

She did. It was one of the most passionately eloquent, if not one of the briefest, letters I ever read.

"I am so glad John received a note from you mentioning my name," she began, and for seven neatly handwritten pages, she let the Reverend Dr. Jerry Falwell, pastor of

Thomas Road Baptist Church, chancellor of Liberty Baptist College, and president of the Moral Majority, have it squarely between the eyes. She ripped him up one side and down the other for maligning a good and honest man whom she had known since we were teenagers by telling outright lies about him on a national television network.

One by one, she took up his statements and refuted them. My "hard letter" to the congregation of First Presbyterian Church, she said, was not a bitter reprisal at all. It was "an open interview" written in response to an elder's plea to know why the church couldn't hold ministers longer than it did, and it "was written out of concern for the people and their next minister." Copies of it were laid on a table in the narthex, and people were free to pick them up or leave them, as they pleased.

"John had no row at the church," she wrote, "and only left because he felt his job was finished. Bitterness isn't on the menu for John's daily diet. I have known him since childhood, and I've never met a more loving, gentle, and caring person. . . . Hate, deception, and revenge have no home in his being."

She also let him know that Jackson had informed me of the arrangement to have him on the day after I was there, so his story to his congregation the next Sunday—"Suddenly the radio is on and here's Dr. Killinger with me going through his garbage, and tapping his telephone, and with me burning his mail. So I called Michael Jackson and said I would like to be on tomorrow, and I was"—was nothing but an out-and-out lie.

"You and John," she concluded her letter, "will ultimately end up like everyone else, with a headstone that records your names, dates of birth, and dates of death. The only acclaim that is important then is a nod from God that he finds acceptable what was accomplished for him between the dates. I can truly hear him say to John, 'Well done, thou *good* and *faithful* servant.'"

The implication was clear: Jerry Falwell was neither of these.

She showed me the letter before she sent it. I think she believed I would say, "You can't send that!" But I didn't.

"I don't think we'll ever hear from Jerry again," I said.

And I was right. Well, almost right. But that's another story.

The gossip about Falwell's remarks on the *Michael Jackson Show* soon died down and we got on with the business of running one of the most difficult churches on God's green earth. I didn't talk about the TV evangelists and the fundamentalists in my sermons in L.A. People in that area watched Schuller's *The Hour of Power,* but they also watched a maverick TV minister named Dr. Gene Scott, a balmy guy with a beard who sat wearing a panama hat and smoking a cigar as he schmoozed about the Gospel, and they watched a very sincere Pentecostalist at the Church on the Way named Dr. Jack Hayford, with whom I became friends my last year in L.A. and later shared the authorship of a book. Some also watched Dr. Lloyd Ogilvie, at Hollywood Presbyterian

Church, with whom I occasionally lunched, and who later became chaplain of the U.S. Senate. They weren't hooked into a particular mode of looking at things, the way TV audiences back in the East had been, and I no longer felt compelled to take up cudgels against what passed for religious programming. I had enough to do, trying to instill some Christian understanding and ideals in my own congregation.

It was a wild ride. Back in the Great Depression era, when the congregation had just erected its magnificent church on the model of Magdalene College in Oxford University and had almost gone bankrupt, a tall, self-confident preacher from Michigan named James Fifield was called as their pastor and accepted the call on the condition that he have total, unconditional freedom to do whatever he wanted to save their bacon. He had his own radio program in Michigan that was bringing in $150,000 annually—a sum probably greater, considering the cost-of-living adjustment, than most TV evangelists make in our own time. Fifield came in and, with characteristic brazenness, met with the bank directors who held the church's note, assured them they would be paid every penny they were owed, and then announced: "But first, gentlemen, we need to borrow another million dollars!"

Incredibly, the directors huddled and agreed to let him have the money.

He used it to hire a large new staff, buy himself a chauffeured limousine, and join the most exclusive social clubs in Los Angeles. He also built a mansion for himself that he later sold to Muhammad Ali. He paid off the original debt in a year and the larger, new one in about four years, and established himself as king on the hill, the undisputed master of the church and its programs. A shallow man theologically, he developed a large, eager congregation through his skillful bullying and the finesse with which he courted the wealthy citizens of Los Angeles.

For example, there was a widow named Mrs. Seaver who gave a vast sum of money to Pepperdine University for a theater center and a lovely boulevard by which to approach it, and Fifield went after her to build an educational wing for First Congregational Church. Part of his deal with her when she contributed the money was that she would become a member of the church's board of trustees. She attended board meetings faithfully for several years. Then one night there was a particularly heated debate over some contentious subject, with a vote taken after the debate. The vote was so close that one of the men on the board turned to Mrs. Seaver and said, "No, Mrs. Seaver, you cannot vote this time. You are only Dr. Fifield's honorary member of this board and you aren't really entitled to a vote."

In the 1950s, when the Cold War was beginning and Senator McCarthy was holding his famous anti-communist hearings in Washington, Fifield started the Freedom Club at First Congregational Church and invited monthly speakers who included McCarthy, Barry Goldwater, and other staunchly conservative figures. The club was enormously popular, and the church reached its highest enrollment during this period.

When Fifield finally had to lay down his scepter, it

created a dramatic power vacuum in the church. He proposed one of his associate ministers as the heir apparent to his throne, but turned on the man once he was installed and undercut him so badly that he could not lead the congregation. Several prominent attorneys banded together to create a cabal that essentially ran the church for decades to come. They controlled not only church policies and major decisions, but numerous church properties as well, including a large cemetery, several apartment buildings, and a 250-acre campground in the mountains at Big Bear, California, a growing resort area.

The history of the pastoral ministry at First Congregational Church between then and the time when I became senior minister was a dark and bloody one, with one minister hounded to a nervous breakdown, another driven off and pursued vengefully by powerful enemies in the church, and most of the others reduced to a level of almost total ineffectiveness. Virtually leaderless, with the cabal in charge of finances, the congregation existed in a state of hostility and generally open warfare.

I mention all of this to say that I found the faith of the congregation, when I arrived, in a complete shambles. Contrary to church members in the East, who appeared to care deeply about whatever theological stance they identified with, the people of Los Angeles as a whole seemed neither to care about theology nor to wish to learn about it. My new congregation was a microcosm of this abysmal lack of Christian understanding. Assaying the situation, I realized I had become the minister of a church that in some ridiculous way mirrored the situation of the fundamentalists in Lynch-burg. That is, the people had been accustomed to the kind of ecclesiastical dictatorship that had been so successful un-der Falwell, and, at the same time, they were as far from hav-ing spiritual depth and discernment as the people at Thomas Road Baptist Church!

My disposition would not allow me to become a new Fi-field, ruling the congregation with anything like the ruth-lessness he displayed, even if my conception of the church had permitted it. I set out to out-Congregationalize the Congregationalists by insisting that important decisions be made by the people of the church—*all* the people of the church and not merely the old ruling cabal—and by trying to democratize the various boards and committees of the church. And at the same time I set about educating my new congregation in the essential elements of the Christian faith.

Not long after I arrived and determined the lay of the land, I commenced an important sermon series on the Apostles' Creed. Congregationalists, being Dissenters in En-gland, had never held to creeds at all, so that our congrega-tion in particular, exhibiting this aversion in spades, had become so theologically neutral—I almost said "theologi-cally ignorant," which would not have been far from the mark—that it could not be said to be guided by any real principles of faith and understanding. I did not attempt to din the Apostles' Creed into them, or insist that new mem-bers accept it in order to join the church, but I did remind them that there is a historical dimension to every faith and that Christians who do not know their own history cannot claim to be Christian in the highest and most beautiful sense.

The church grew under my leadership—we always had very healthy new communicants' classes—and I gradually began to believe that I had earned my spurs as a fiscal and political leader in addition to having a place as pastor and preacher. Gradually we recaptured some of our standing in the larger community of Los Angeles, attracting new members from the business, social, and artistic elements of the society. We drew huge crowds from the mid-Wilshire area for our annual Thanksgiving services, which, with the Honorable Tom Bradley's cooperation, we renamed the Mayor's Thanksgiving Service. With the help of ABC Television, we commenced a powerful literacy effort called Project Literacy Los Angeles (PLLA), and had Barbara Bush, the newly elected president's wife, as our special guest on its first Sunday. We took a major leadership role in establishing Help-Net, Inc., a citywide organization designed to provide food, shelter, legal assistance, and other necessities to the community's growing population of poor and homeless. In short, we tried in every way possible to become Christ to our neighbors in the City of Angels.

At the same time, I became a regular columnist for the *Los Angeles Times* and the *Los Angeles Herald Examiner,* and made a lot of one-minute meditations on life and religion that were broadcast over a number of local radio stations during the hectic morning and afternoon commutation hours. I was active in the Mid-Wilshire Priests, Ministers, and Rabbis Association, and continued to fly all over the

United States on a frequent basis to speak at ministers' conferences, as well as to conduct preaching seminars for U.S. military chaplains in Europe and the Orient. In addition to all this, I developed an extensive counseling practice, meeting regularly with all kinds of people, from street dwellers to prominent writers, doctors, and attorneys.

Looking back on those years, I wonder that I found the energy for all I had to do, and that I didn't simply have a nervous breakdown like one of my predecessors a few years earlier. (Wouldn't Falwell have loved that!) But it was a happy, golden time in spite of my frenetic schedule and the fact that I never did feel that the congregation developed a significant sense of love and spirituality. We made many warm, wonderful friendships that have continued to this day, and had many exciting adventures, meeting TV and movie stars, dining with power brokers, and hugging street people.

While I thought very little about Jerry Falwell and his further exploits back in Lynchburg, my life as a minister and a theologian was continuing to be formed by my encounter with him during those six years I had spent in his town. It was the frightening lack of real theological content in his messages and his work with the Moral Majority that had compelled me to assess my own theology and ask whether it was up to the task of helping to shape a truly godly society in our time.

When I look now at the sermons I preached in those years in Los Angeles, I realize how much stronger and more vital my preaching was than it could possibly have become if I hadn't encountered Falwell during our Lynchburg years. Among the widely varied topics I see are "The Nourishing Quiet," "Jesus in a Plain Brown Wrapper," "Dying of Thirst at the Edge of the River," "The Astounding Event at the Heart of Faith," "Recovering Wonder," "The Scandal of Our Faith," "The Simplest Creed of All," "The Great Importance of Little Deeds," and "The Church That God Wants."

Every sermon, I like to think, was like a small arc on a circle, connected directly by its radii to the very heart and center of the Christian faith. Every one was theologically grounded in a historical understanding of Christianity, yet fresh and applicable as the morning newspaper. In addition to the series of sermons I preached on the Apostles' Creed, which I've mentioned, I preached a series on prayer, one on the Beatitudes, and another on the greatest teachings of Jesus.

Lloyd Holzgraf, our organist, said he had been playing the organ at First Congregational Church for twenty-five years, and had heard more from the pulpit about Jesus while I was there than he had heard in all the rest of the years put together.

Maybe this wasn't entirely because of my brushes with Falwell and the other TV evangelists, but a lot of it was owing to them. The popular pulpit in America was offering people a holy mishmash—a pablum concocted of one part truisms and two parts self-centeredness, with bits and pieces of fundamentalist theology and moral judgment thrown in—and I felt as never before in my life the necessity of preaching sermons filled with truth, honesty, and the lively spirit of God.

Being the minister of the First Congregational Church was the most demanding job I had ever had. Merely staying alive in Los Angeles is a full-time job in itself. But staying alive and pastoring a church as much at odds with itself as that one proved to be totally enervating. When I had a chance to take a day off, Anne and I usually drove down to Laguna Beach or Dana Point and walked along the ocean. I remember saying to her more than once, "If I don't get out of here soon, I'll be carried out in a pine box!"

So when an invitation came from Dr. Thomas Corts, president of Samford University in Birmingham, Alabama, to become a Distinguished Professor of Religion and Culture with the rare freedom to teach any subject I wished, the way only one or two of my old professors had ever been able to do, it seemed to be a passport from heaven. Samford had been given $50 million to build a new ecumenical divinity school, and I could participate in the development of that shining new enterprise. I looked forward to teaching creative writing and theology and literature in the English department as well, but it was the chance to work in a divinity school that really stirred my enthusiasm.

I was greeted at Samford with a great deal of publicity, pomp, and circumstance. I spoke each morning to the faculty and administrative officers assembled for a preschool workshop. My photograph was inserted next to the dean's in an expensive new monograph published for the divinity school, and was as large as his, while the photographs of other professors were smaller and brought up the rear. I marched at the head of the divinity school procession and preached to the university student body. There were articles about me in all the local newspapers and magazines. I was invited to serve on the board of the Alabama Humanities Foundation, the Alabama arm of the National Endowment for the Arts and Humanities, and to speak at the pastors' conference of the next Southern Baptist Convention meeting.

Samford was a Baptist university, and part of the satisfaction I felt in accepting a teaching post there was the sense of having grown up as a Baptist and returning to repay some of the debt I owed to my origins. For the first time in years, I was being invited to preach in large Baptist churches across the South. It felt good to get back to my roots, and to preach and teach in a denomination that was going through all kinds of growing pains.

But I had not reckoned with the jealousy and unkindness of the man who had become dean of the divinity school, Dr. Timothy George. George had earned his Th.D. at Harvard Divinity School under a professor I had loved and revered, the great church historian George Huntston Williams. I had enormous respect for that. I knew he was much more conservative than I was, but didn't consider that a problem. We were in a university setting, and I saw no reason we couldn't both be open-minded.

I was wrong. Only one of us was.

I had been promised that I could teach any subject I wished, in any department of the university. In my conversations with the president and provost of the university, it had always been understood that I would teach preaching, which was the field in which I had taught at Vanderbilt

University. I was a nationally known preacher, I had published textbooks on preaching and worship, I was on the editorial board of a premier preaching magazine, and I spoke to ministers' conferences all over the United States and abroad on the subject of preaching. But Dean George said I could not teach the basic courses in preaching because he had a fundamentalist professor on the faculty whom he preferred to do it.

The tensions between George and me mounted steadily. I invited him to lunch several times, hoping to improve our relationship, but it was useless. He was extremely conservative in his theology, he was a friend of Jerry Falwell and other fundamentalist leaders, and he was eager to become an important figure in conservative religious circles. I was therefore restricted to teaching small, upper-level seminars, and, I soon learned, students were warned to avoid my courses lest they become contaminated by my liberal spirit.

In December 1992, when I had been at Samford three and a half years, I went to Oxford for a one-semester sabbatical leave in order to do research for a book. Sometime in the spring of 1993, I received a communication from the editor of the student newspaper at Samford indicating that Jerry Falwell had been on the campus to address the Cumberland School of Law. I have no idea why the law school might have invited him to speak, unless it was to give the students an opportunity of visiting with the man who had almost single-handedly united the country's evangelicals and fundamentalists to change the direction of American politics, and, with it, American law and justice as well.

During a question-and-answer period after one of his speeches, said the editor, Falwell was asked about my opposition to his ministry during my years in Lynchburg. Falwell's immediate response, reported in an article in the student newspaper, was that he didn't understand how a Christian university like Samford could have a man like me on its faculty.

I laughed at this, because I regarded it as the dying growl of an old enemy who was no longer relevant in my life. I had not heard any more from him since Anne had written him that time in Los Angeles, and had assumed that that part of our lives was over a long time ago. He had made his grab for the helm of the *PTL Club,* had been repudiated by the right wing of his own support group, and had been exposed as a Judas by the Bakkers, who said he conned them out of their program by pretending that Jimmy Swaggart was set to take over the *PTL Club* and that he would disappoint Swaggart by assuming the manager's role for Jim Bakker until his release from prison. His popularity with voters had sunk so low that no self-respecting candidate for office wanted his support, and he was increasingly regarded, both in Lynchburg and in the nation as a whole, as a historical anomaly, a man who had become famous for getting in front of a movement and had then lacked whatever it took to remain there. As I said, I wondered why he had been invited to speak to the law school, but promptly forgot about the matter.

When we returned from England in the summer, our flight didn't arrive in Birmingham until midnight. We were quite surprised, therefore, to find a small party of friends, including three or four professors and a secretary from the divinity school, waiting to greet us. We hugged and kissed and said inane things about the lateness of the hour and everybody's having to be at work in the morning, and, once we had got our luggage, departed for home.

When I went to the divinity school a couple of days later to check my messages, read my mail, and take care of any business that needed minding, I learned something that explained our friends' presence at the airport that late at night. Sometime after Falwell's visit to Samford, Dean George had ordered my name and classes deleted from the divinity school computers. Moreover, the divinity school was being relocated in a newly renovated building elsewhere on campus and I had not been assigned an office in the posh new quarters. Instead, I was to be housed in a musty old office in the undergraduate department of religion, where the ancient gray carpets were grossly stained by radiator leaks and an eerie painting of a Hebrew scapegoat, its head still bearing the crimson where it was marked by the high priest with the sins of the people before being driven into the wilderness, was the only adornment on the walls!

Our friends knew what had happened and were a hundred percent sympathetic with us. They had not known how to phone or write and tell us in advance of our arrival home, but they wanted to show their solidarity with us by being there to meet us, even at an ungodly hour.

I have always regarded my deletion from the divinity school's teaching roster as Falwell's parting shot. I cannot prove that he and Dean George sat down together and planned my banishment from the new divinity school, but it is hard for me to believe they didn't. George had often bragged that he appeared with Falwell on the *Old-Time Gospel Hour,* and if they didn't conspire in my expulsion from the divinity school, I'm certain that George at least took his cue from his fundamentalist mentor and did what he did knowing he had his support.

I made friends with the scapegoat, and actually became quite fond of it. We seemed to share a common fate. I was sixty years old when this happened, and didn't have the will and energy to relocate. I protested, of course, to President Corts and the university provost, Dr. William Hull, who had known about Dean George's action and had even discussed it with him. But they were too worried about George's support—and Falwell's!—among fundamentalist Baptists in Alabama to overrule his decision.

I brought a lawsuit against the university for permitting a rogue administrator to violate the understanding under which I had accepted a position at Samford, but the federal judge in Birmingham threw out the case on the grounds that Samford was a religious institution and he could not adjudicate a legal matter in which the state would be infringing on its rights. My attorneys, whom I remember as extraordinarily decent gentlemen, filed an appeal, but the same three federal judges in Atlanta who in 2000 would rule for the Republican party in the matter of the election results in Florida upheld the Birmingham verdict. When the attorneys considered the makeup of the U.S. Supreme Court—a court that Jerry Falwell's influence in the 1980s had helped to shape—they regarded our chances of having the appeals court decision overturned as extremely unlikely, and counseled dropping the suit.

So I remained at Samford another two years, teaching in the English and religion departments, and, when I could begin drawing social security, retired. I continued to be busy with my writing and traveling, and at some point during these final years wrote a novel called *The Counting House,* about an unscrupulous TV evangelist. The only agent I showed it to didn't like it because she said it was "sad and sordid," so I stuck it in a closet, where it remains to this day.

The chairman of the department of religion during my final years at Samford was Dr. Bill J. Leonard, who later became the dean of a fine new divinity school at Wake Forest University in North Carolina. Bill, a slight man with a perennially smiling face and lilting voice, hailed originally from Texas and still spoke with the characteristic vigor and color of the Lone Star State. One day we were sitting in his office chatting when the subject of Falwell's visit to the campus and my subsequent banishment from the divinity school came up in the conversation.

His eyes twinkling with devilment, Bill said, "That man's been like gum on your shoe, hasn't he? You stepped on him once and you've been tracking him ever since!"

He was right.

I don't regret it. Jerry Falwell was a strong, fascinating individual, and whenever you become involved with somebody like that it changes your life, whether you want it to or not. That's what Jack Burden felt about Willie Stark, the fictional character representing Huey Long in Robert Penn Warren's novel *All the King's Men*. Once he had met Stark, his life would never be the same, because it became unavoidably tangled up with Stark's.

I think that's why Anne and I felt sad, in our different ways, about Falwell's death. We had become entangled with him, and part of our own lives had died when he did.

Epilogue

The Great Divider

Nobody is more of a pariah than last year's celebrity.

I didn't see much of Falwell's funeral on television, but I regretted that a lot of the people I thought should be there weren't. James Dobson and Ralph Reed both lauded him on *Larry King Live,* and I could tell Larry mourned the loss of somebody he had enjoyed interviewing several times across the years. But I don't know if they came to the funeral. Franklin Graham was there, and I'm sure a few other luminaries of the religious world.

But it seemed especially tawdry of the White House to send some second- or third-level functionary to represent an administration that probably owed its very existence to Falwell's efforts, even though it only rode in on the tail end of the evangelical-fundamentalist coalition he helped to create. George W. Bush was so low in the polls that it wouldn't have hurt him and Laura to come. It would have made a more fitting send-off for an old warrior who had eagerly sought and gained a seat of honor at several presidential inaugurations.

Social historians will be sifting the evidence for decades to come, but I can't help thinking that in their final analysis my old friend and nemesis will occupy a place of considerable importance. It was an enormously important time, after all, when the whole nation, and not just the nation but the entire world, was realigning itself along the two sides of a very deep gulf. There had always been conservatives and liberals—Cain and Abel may have been their earliest representatives—but in the last third of the twentieth century there seemed to be something at work, like an irresistible electromagnetic force, driving them apart with a vengeance.

For Americans, the long, debilitating struggle in Vietnam may have triggered it. The fears and anxieties of the Cold War era also contributed something. Who can forget the baleful influence of Senator Joseph McCarthy, the self-righteous saber rattling of Senator Barry Goldwater, or all the Young Republican clubs on university campuses? But it was the popular uprisings against the war in Vietnam—the hippie movement and free love and draft-card rebellions—that frightened a lot of middle-class citizens into the arms of right-wing groups promising to save the world from the threat of impending chaos.

And there he was, that irrepressible crusader from Lynchburg, offering hope and salvation to everybody who would take part in his battle to recapture America for God, morality, and fundamentalist religion. He must have looked like a true messiah to millions of Americans who were sick and tired of wishy-washy religion and namby-pamby politicians. Bold and intrepid, filled with self-righteous energy, he offered a way forward—albeit through the rearview mirror—and used his emphatic oratory to make it look like a future that shop workers and truck drivers and grade-school teachers could unite to possess. In a world where everything was shifting and changing, he offered the hope of shelter and stability.

Others were preaching a similar message—Pat Robertson, Charles Stanley, Kenneth Copeland, Oral Roberts, and half the cinder-block tabernacle preachers in America—but none of them stood out the way Falwell did. He had a styleless style. What he lacked in class he made up for in predictability, shrillness, and self-assurance. His voice rang out loudly and clearly above the crowd, like that of the most exotic and jaded barker at a carnival: "Right this way, folks, to a safer, more God-fearing world! That's right! Hurry into the tent! The big show's about to begin and you don't want to miss it!"

There wasn't anything original about Falwell except himself. His church was like any other storefront church that eventually acquires its own nondescript building. His school was a poor, struggling imitation of Bob Jones University. His TV programming was like that of any other old-time gospel hour. His preaching was third-rate and a lot of it came straight out of old fundamentalist textbooks. But he was loud and persistent, and he wasn't afraid to pick a fight with anybody.

I often thought of him as a street brawler. He liked picking on people and groups, and if there was anything he liked better than that, it was to be picked on himself, so he could holler and squeal and claim he was being attacked. He loved those quarrels with *Penthouse* and *Hustler.* It gave him stature in his congregation to be ill-treated by what he called "evil, pornographic magazines." He was truculent and he was a bully. He swaggered around the school yard threatening anybody who even looked like a competitor. He bragged about his fights, whether he won or lost. He gloried in his scars and his reputation as a combatant.

I don't really believe Falwell invented the coalition of evangelical and fundamentalist forces he is sometimes credited with forming, I think it was on the way to happening whether he had been on the scene or not. But he was clever enough, when he heard the band oompahing down the street, to grab a baton and get ahead of it, and then it was his, whether he had anything to do with organizing it or not. This is the way he was with the *PTL Club* when he took it over. It didn't matter that it was the thriving brainchild of Jim and Tammy Bakker and they had put years into shaping and nurturing it; when he got hold of the microphone in front of their audience, it became his dog-and-pony show, not theirs.

Yet it was important for Jerry Falwell to come along when he did and provide the titular leadership he bestowed on the conservative movement. If he hadn't done it, someone like him would have had to be invented, and it probably wouldn't have been anyone with half his sassiness and color.

Falwell was a genius at producing division. His boasting, his haranguing, his masterful use of paranoia—reminding people that the world was against them—were all part of his shtick. The entire world was already beginning to divide along fault lines that lay deep in the human situation— fundamentalism was far more than an American phenomenon, as studies of world religions have shown—but he leapt into the fray with a talent for expediting things, for reminding people of why they hated one another and what they ought to do about it.

Falwell's mouth was both his finest asset and his greatest liability. No one who ever saw or heard him will ever forget his cockiness and self-assurance; his ability to talk about biblical things he didn't understand as if he had written them himself; his confidence in his pronouncements on everything from Teletubbies to Supreme Court rulings; his way of thrusting his right index finger boldly into the air as if it were the mighty digit of Yahweh himself, ready to divide the waters or lower the boom on a sinful nation; and the ringing tones of his full-bodied voice, which he learned to project forcefully to the last row of a movie theater in the years before his church could afford an amplifying system.

There was an awful joke that went around Lynchburg during my years there, to the effect that Falwell had died and the undertaker was worried because he didn't have a casket large enough to hold the body.

"Don't worry," said his wife, Macel. "Just give him an enema and he'll fit in a shoe box!"

Having seen him on television a few times during his last years, when he had blimped up like a zeppelin, I couldn't help remembering this execrable story after he died. I didn't want to remember it, because it made me think, "Shame on you! That's no way to remember somebody who has just died!" But like some ridiculous tune you try to forget, it kept cycling and recycling through my head.

Why was this? Was there some truth in the image? Did I think he really was full of sanctimonious crap?

In a way, I suppose that's what it was. The story, horrible as it was, pinpointed the enigma of Jerry Falwell. A lot of the man was only sanctimonious crap. He bragged, blustered, and shot off his mouth, he pirouetted through life like a linebacker for the Pittsburgh Steelers tripping through a child's birthday party. And yet, in spite of this, there was something there to respect, to stand in awe of, the way one would stand in awe of Rosie Greer in a tutu. Most people who knew him—at least, most of the people *I* knew who knew him—made fun of him or laughed at him behind his back, yet still looked on him as some kind of miracle they were privileged to behold.

Jim Price and I were talking about this recently. "You know," said Jim, "most people knew him as this loud, bombastic figure who didn't have a sensitive bone in his body. Yet he could be very kind and gentle too."

Jim remembered a funeral he had conducted, when the family wanted Falwell to "say a few words" as well. It was in the winter, and there had been snow on the ground. Several times, Falwell had driven his four-wheeler up to the widow's house and taken her to the hospital to visit her husband while he was dying.

"Most people never knew that about Jerry," said Jim, "but he could be a decent man when he wanted to."

Paul Prather, a columnist for Kentucky's *Lexington Herald,* said as much, but in an inverted way: "It wasn't that I disagreed with everything he said, although I disagreed with much of it. Still, Falwell was a Christian; I'm a Christian. I shared some of his core beliefs." The problem, said Prather, was that Falwell came across as "a narrow man, tightly wound," who "sounded angry, self-aggrandizing and dismissive of those who didn't share his views." So, while Prather respected part of who Falwell was, there was something about his manner that put him off.

Perhaps Bishop John Shelby Spong has expressed it as well as anybody: "He represented everything that repels me about religion. He was closed-minded, bigoted and abusive as religious people tend to be when they believe that they possess God's truth. Yet, I never disliked this man. He tapped into something in the American psyche that, had he not done so, I believe, someone else, perhaps worse, would have."

That's precisely it: Falwell touched something in the American psyche that made him what he was. If he hadn't been a preacher, he would have become one of the best used-car salesmen in Hoboken or one of the biggest gamblers at Atlantic City or one of the most flamboyant presidential candidates the Republican Party has ever seen. But he was a preacher, and as a preacher he made contact with something in the average American soul of the last half of the twentieth century—the John and Jane Does of media-land—that seemed to shout back, "Amen! Preach on, brother, that's the way it is!"

It was an apocalyptic time, with America and the USSR in a nuclear arms race; with people competing to have the fastest cars and biggest houses on the block; with gays and lesbians coming out of the closet; with marriages failing and homes breaking up at alarming rates; with educational systems disintegrating and fourth graders on mind-altering drugs; with twelve- and fourteen-year-old girls getting pregnant and abortions being performed virtually on demand; with groaning, overcrowded sports stadiums and dismal, half-empty churches; and with political leaders who had virtually given up on the possibility of a workable future, much less on convincing people to follow them into it. And here came this strident voice in the cultural wilderness, the carny barker shouting, "This way! This way! Don't miss the big show!"

It was no wonder that people followed, came to his rallies, mailed in their donations, and bought what this Pied Piper in a black suit with a bright tie and a "Jesus First" pin in his lapel was trying to sell. Nor was it any wonder that one devoted supporter, a Mrs. Faye Francis of Route 1, Forest, Virginia, wrote to the Lynchburg newspaper about Falwell on May 4, 1981, that "if ever any man who ever breathed will occupy the right hand of God the Father, it is he."

For many people, like this dear lady, he was the savior sent by the Almighty. Never mind Jesus. She had heard Jerry Falwell.

As for yours truly, well, I guess Falwell would say I have spent the time since we were together making my way down "the slippery slope." He might even say I have been *plummeting* down it, the way he cascaded fully clothed down that giant water slide in the photograph of him at *PTL Club*'s Heritage USA.

After leaving Samford University—thanks, Jerry!—I spent several summers as minister of the Little Stone Church on Mackinac Island, Michigan, a lovely resort destination near the Canadian border, and used the rest of my time to think and write and speak in various places. The theological mind Falwell had set in motion kept agitating about things that seemed important, such as who Jesus really was and what he intended the church to be, if indeed he intended anything at all for it; what made Christians behave the way they did, as if God had put them exclusively in charge of the world and all its inmates; what globalized faith might look like, if we ever get to that point; and, in the meantime, what we ought to know about other faiths, in order to be ready when we do get there.

I wrote a book defending J. K. Rowling's Harry Potter stories against preachers like Falwell, who said there were too many witches and wizards in them for tender young imaginations. I wrote a book called *Ten Things I Learned Wrong from a Conservative Church* that got me in trouble in my hometown, because the conservative church I was talking about was the one I grew up in. My old minister in those days would have worshiped Falwell. And I wrote another book called *Seven Things They Don't Teach You in Seminary,* because I wanted to warn young ministers about the way institutional churches will eat them alive and then spit out their bones if they aren't exceedingly careful.

My most recent book is called *The Changing Shape of Our Salvation.* In it, I trace the history of the Christian faith from its origins in Judaism through the early church to the Middle Ages and beyond. Then I talk about how all the developments in world culture and society since the 1950s—especially TV and the computer and electronic communications—have forced a transformation in how most Christians now regard what it means to be saved. Instead of "pie in the sky by and by," as traditional salvation has sometimes been defined, they talk in terms of personal fulfillment and a meaningful life in this world. Even Billy Graham, the iconic evangelist, I pointed out, has softened his stance in his latter years, and admits that Muslims, Jews, Hindus, and Buddhists may be allowed into heaven.

I suggested to my editors at the publishing company that they send a copy of that book to Jerry Falwell when it appeared. It would have been my final nod to my old friend and enemy from Lynchburg. But unfortunately he died before the publication date.

I was already writing books before I met Falwell, but not the kind of books I write now. He was absolutely right about the slippery slope. Sometimes I wonder how long it will be before I reach the bottom. Other times I think I might keep slipping forever. I wonder how he knew about this anyway.

It doesn't matter. I was only one of many people whose lives he touched in one way or another. He had heft, and not just the kind that won't fit in a shoe box. I mean genuine *heft,* as in weight, purpose, gravity. *Gravity* may be the right word. Not *gravitas,* that's something else. Gravity as in what planets have, what the sun has, what inevitably draws things toward them and out of their own orbits. Gravity can suck you in and carry you away before you know it.

His gravity did that. I didn't see it coming. I never expected to be affected by it. But I was, and in retrospect I have to honor him for it.

Farewell, Jerry. I honestly wish we could have been real friends.